Accession no.
01055062

The Churc

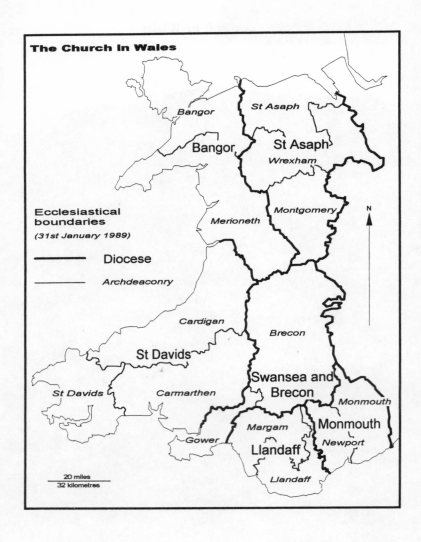

The Church in Wales

Bangor

St Asaph

Bangor

St Asaph

Wrexham

Ecclesiastical
boundaries

(31st January 1989)

——————— Diocese

——————— Archdeaconry

Merioneth

Montgomery

N

Cardigan

Brecon

St Davids

St Davids

Carmarthen

Swansea and
Brecon

Monmouth

Gower

Margam

Monmouth

Newport

Llandaff

Llandaff

20 miles
32 kilometres

The Church in Wales

THE SOCIOLOGY OF A TRADITIONAL INSTITUTION

CHRIS HARRIS and RICHARD STARTUP

· 127 1969

LIBRARY

ACC. NO. 01055062

DEPT. r

CLASS NO. 262.03429 HAR

UNIVERSITY COLLEGE CHESTER

UNIVERSITY OF WALES PRESS
CARDIFF
1999

© Chris Harris and Richard Startup, 1999

British Library Cataloguing-in-Publication Data
A catalogue record for this book is available from the British Library

ISBN 0-7083-1575-5 (paperback)
     0-7083-1574-7 (hardback)

Al rights reserved. No part of this book may be reproduced, stored in a retrieval system, or transmitted, in any form or by any means, electronic, mechanical, photocopying, recording or otherwise, without clearance from the University of Wales Press, 6 Gwennyth Street, Cardiff, CF2 4YD.

Typeset at Action Publishing Technology, Gloucester
Printed in Great Britain by Dinefwr Press, Llandybïe

Contents

Maps

Tables

Preface

British mainstream Churches have experienced a decline in membership in recent decades. How should they respond? The Department of Sociology and Anthropology of the University of Wales Swansea was asked to design a study to enable an assessment to be made of the 'state of the Church in Wales'. The results of the study were later reported to the Church's Governing Body. Towards the end of the data-collection period, the then Archbishop of Wales expressed the hope that it would be possible for the data gathered to be fully presented in the form of academic publications. This book is the most recent of a series of academic publications arising from the study. The data it produced help to provide an account of the predicament of the Anglican Church in Wales which we believe will interest all those concerned with the position of Christianity in contemporary society. To prepare for the future, one must understand the past; this is especially so for the members of a traditional institution. Initially a brief outline of the recent history of the Church in Wales is provided, together with a description of its composition. However, the main body of this work consists of a sociological analysis of the Church in Wales, with particular reference to the 1990s. It is on this basis that the prospects for the Church are evaluated in the light of its structure and membership and the rapidly changing society in which it finds itself.

Though no longer established, the Church in Wales retains the mission of an established church in a society which is secular and whose culture is postmodern. Though not an 'organization' but a moral community, it none the less has organization which is both hierarchical and territorial. Part One provides the first ever description and analysis of the territorial organization of a church and demonstrates the way in which the resulting resource distribution tends to reinforce the traditional emphasis on maintenance rather than mission. Part Two of the study, by contrast, focuses on the beliefs, attitudes and activities of members of the Church, both clerical and lay, and the way in which the attitudes of the clergy and the characteristics of the laity impose severe limitations on the extent to which their devotion and talents can be mobilized for mission. Part Three provides a wide-ranging discussion of the conclusions of the study, centring on the problems posed for religious belief and witness in a postmodern culture and the barriers to change deriving from traditional organization.

The assemblage of data drawn upon is distinctive in several ways. A survey of benefices provides the opportunity for analysis of Church structure at provincial, diocesan and parish levels. In this connection a classification of benefices plays a central role. Various differences within and between dioceses are identified, particularly on the rural–urban dimension. In addition, the perspectives of clerical and lay members are explored using the complementary sources of attitude surveys and reports of discussions in deaneries and parochial church councils. On this basis one can evaluate the effectiveness with which the Church organizes to achieve its goals given the available human and material resources. The significance of the 'State of the Church' study is that it supplied to the Church the single most valuable compendium of information about itself for enabling it meaningfully to frame its various responses to the problems and challenges of contemporary British society. However, many of those problems, and the nature of the challenges they pose to the Welsh Church as an institution, are perennial, and it is these enduring problems and challenges that constitute the theme of this investigation.

The purpose of the present work is to further our understanding of the nature and contemporary predicament of an extraordinarily diverse, complex and changing major Welsh institution and thereby to make a more general contribution to the sociology of religion. It is hoped that the approach may be characterized as both sympathetic and sociologically rigorous, and the analysis is if anything enhanced by the fact that one of us is an insider, the other an outsider, with respect to the Church. It is believed that the study will be of interest to teachers and students of sociology, religion and Welsh society, to members of the Anglican Church and of other Christian Churches, and to a still wider public seeking to understand the changing nature of organized religion within contemporary society.

Chris Harris and Richard Startup

1

Introduction

Perhaps the very term 'Celtic Church' gives rise to confusion, for it was in fact an integral part of the universal Church ... Indeed, it would be better to describe it as the Church among the speakers of Celtic languages.

John Davies, *A History of Wales*, 1993, 72

Sociologists, like historians, are used to grappling with phenomena which lack clear definition. Much of their subject-matter does not afford them the certainties available to those who restrict their studies to legal and political institutions. None the less, their field includes phenomena which do have institutional form.

Unlike 'the Celtic Church', the Church in Wales indubitably exists as a distinct entity: it is 'by law established', since it came into being as a result of the Welsh Church Act of 1914 (Davies 1970). However, what that Act effected was its disestablishment. What was disestablished when the 1914 Act came into effect in 1920 was nevertheless not a distinct Church but, rather, an integral part of the Church of England. What had legal form before that date was not one entity ('the Welsh Church') but four: the dioceses of St Asaph, Bangor, St Davids and Llandaff in the Province of Canterbury. Prior to its disestablishment the Welsh Church could perhaps be best described as the Anglican Church among the inhabitants of the Principality of Wales. It was therefore the representatives of the four Welsh dioceses that met together in October 1917 in Cardiff to establish the governance of the new body that the Welsh Church Act had called into existence.

The 1914 Act did not strictly create the Welsh Anglican Church. However, to disestablish the four Welsh dioceses without separating them from the established Church of England would have created an anomalous situation, and Randall

Davidson, the then Archbishop of Canterbury, urged upon the Welsh bishops that they should constitute the four dioceses as a separate province of the Anglican Communion (Walker 1976, 169).

The manner of the disendowment was also such as to necessitate that the Welsh dioceses constitute themselves as a collectivity. The 1914 Act only partially disendowed the four dioceses, but the way this was achieved was by sequestrating all the property previously held by the four dioceses. In the words of one historian of these events:

> on the day on which the . . . Act came into force all the property of the [four dioceses], the cathedrals and churches, the bishops' palaces, deaneries, vicarages and rectories, churchyards, glebe land and endowments, ancient and modern, [were] vested in the Commissioners of Church Temporalities in Wales.   (Price 1990, 8)

However, having sequestered the entire property of the dioceses, the Act then made provision for partially re-endowing them, and this required that they establish a body in which the re-endowments were to be vested.

It is in this sense that the present Church was established by the Act effecting its *dis*establishment. The arrangements for disendowment and re-endowment necessitated that the four dioceses form themselves into the body corporate which became the contemporary 'Church in Wales' and the prime task of the Convention of 1917 was to establish a body corporate to receive back that part of church property from the commissioners with which it was to be re-endowed. The property-holding body that supplied this requirement was termed the Representative Body (RB). The terminology is significant: the body was to represent the interests of the constituent dioceses of the new Church, which are, to this day, bound together by their financial dependence on a central source of revenue.

The 1917 Convention, in addition to setting up the RB, created a Governing Body (GB). The creation of this institution was not directly or indirectly required by the Welsh Church Act, and the Church of England had no such body, being governed at that time by its clerical convocations. Moreover, the proposed governing body was to be concerned with policy rather than property and to comprise the Welsh bishops and elected representatives of both clergy and laity. Hence the proposal was one for the establishment of a system of what is now termed synodical government half a century before it was adopted by the Church of England.

Unsurprisingly, the establishment of this body was more controversial than the establishment of the RB. There was, however, one overriding consideration in its favour. The Convention had before it a number of proposals drawn up by a committee established by the dioceses in 1914 to deal with problems arising from the implementation of the Welsh Church Act. The Convention did not have time to consider all these, and it was necessary to create a body representative of the four dioceses to which the Convention could refer them.

One question which the Convention of 1917 failed to resolve was the name of the future province. It seems likely that the majority sentiment of the Convention favoured 'the Church of Wales'. However, since the Welsh Church Act referred to 'the church in Wales', there was, in Price's words, 'considerable anxiety as to what might be the legal consequences of adopting a different name' (Price 1990, 10). The new GB played safe and chose 'the Church in Wales' in 1921.

The hesitancy over the name has considerable significance for our understanding of the contemporary Church in Wales. In the first place, one of the arguments for disestablishment was that, by contrast to England, the Anglican church in Wales had ceased to be the church of the Welsh people. That the Welsh had become, during the nineteenth century, predominantly Nonconformist was incontrovertible (Williams 1991, 64). However, the argument for disestablishment depended on the contrast to England. While the English had not become Nonconformist, it was far from true that a majority of the English population were adherents of the established Church of England. Whereas in Wales the nineteenth century had seen the growth of Nonconformity, in England it had seen the growth of an urban working class, a class which remained largely outside the established church. As a result, though it was true that the Anglican Church was not the church of the Welsh people, neither, in numerical terms, was the Church of England the church of the English people (Hastings 1991, 40). Indeed, as Davies has pointed out, it is one of the ironies of Welsh disestablishment that 'by the second quarter of the twentieth century, commitment to Anglicanism – measured by the numbers attending Easter Communion – was stronger in Wales than it was in England' (Davies 1993, 539).

Yet no one suggested the disestablishment of the English Church on those grounds. So why not call the Welsh Church 'the Church of Wales'? The argument against calling it the Church *in* Wales did not, however, proceed along these lines and is of considerable sociological interest since it tacitly involved the classic distinction in the sociology of religious groups (Weber 1965; Troeltsch 1981) between 'church' (*ecclesia*), on the one hand, and 'denomination' and 'sect' on the other. Robertson (1970, 120–38) simplified this typology by distinguishing religious bodies on two grounds: whether they are (or claim to be) uniquely legitimate and whether they are inclusive or exclusive. Sects do not claim unique legitimacy and are exclusive; churches claim unique legitimacy and are inclusive.

The Church in Wales clearly claims unique legitimacy inasmuch as, like its sister-church in England, it claims to be the historic Christian Church in its named territory. Its claims to uniqueness are not, however, inconsistent with the title 'Church in Wales'. The problem arises with its inclusive nature. The claim to the title 'Church *of* Wales' does not rest on the empirical claim to be the religious body with the most members or attenders or with the allegiance of a majority of the population. It rests, rather, on its definition of the relationship between itself and that population. Both denominations and sects exist for their members. Churches exist for the inhabitants of their territory, who are either compelled to be members (that is, they have a duty to belong) or regarded as potential members (that is, they have a right to belong).

This takes us on to the issue of establishment. The churchly character of pre-Reformation Christianity derived from the Roman Church being the only Christian body: it was *de facto* unique, and what Weber calls its 'hieratic domination' was supported by those having political domination. The emergence of the modern state coincided with the emergence of Protestantism: that is, the sectarian secession of different Protestant groups from the historic Church. The response of the English state to this situation was to reform the historic Church in an attempt to prevent Protestant secession and to make the reformed Church the official state Church of the English and Welsh people to which all the inhabitants of the territory of the state were deemed to belong by virtue of their birth. By this means it was hoped to avoid the religious strife characteristic of the continental Reformation and to abolish at a stroke the medieval tension between hieratic and political domination. By 'nationalizing' the Church (making it subordinate to the state), this tension was abolished. Political and religious dissent became indistinguishable, and disabilities were placed on dissenters to encourage conformity. Dissenters were also required to continue to support the established church financially through tithes.

By the time of Welsh disestablishment the political disabilities on dissenters had already been removed. Disestablishment of the Welsh Church was, therefore, primarily an economic measure as far as Welsh society was concerned. For the Church it was, in addition, a political measure which removed the four dioceses from state control. In this sense, the Welsh Church became a 'free church'.

The question inevitably arises as to whether, by being severed from the inclusive and compulsory institution of the state, the Welsh Church thereby ceased to have a unique legitimacy and so ceased to be a 'church' as sociologically defined, becoming instead a 'denomination', the Anglican church in Wales, rather than the 'church of Wales'. Behind the desire to adopt the title 'Church of Wales' lie two assumptions which are vitally important in understanding the contemporary Church in Wales.

The first is that by separating from the Province of Canterbury, the Welsh Church did not give up its claim to be the historic Christian Church of Wales. Herein lies the foundation of the claim of Anglicanism in the British Isles to be unique. The second assumption concerns inclusivity. The title 'the (Anglican) Church in Wales' implies Anglicanism among the inhabitants of the Principality. In such a case the Welsh Church is the same kind of religious body as any other denomination, in that it exists as a voluntary association of individuals who have chosen that particular mode of profession of the Christian faith. By contrast, a Church *of* Wales would be a 'church' in the strict sense: that is, either a religious body of which all the inhabitants of Wales are involuntarily members unless they opt out of it, or a religious body which has a duty to provide spiritual care to all the inhabitants of its territory.

The churchly character of a religious body is manifested in a plural and secular society in terms of its residual character rather than its compulsory status. As Davies has put it succinctly:

> In spite of disestablishment, the Anglicans held to the principle that they had a responsibility to parishioners in their entirety. Indeed, as they retained possession of the parish churches and cathedrals, they continued to look like an Establishment – and to a considerable extent be treated like one.   (Davies 1993, 539)

As sociologists, we prefer a different terminology from that of the historian, while endorsing the general point that he makes. We would prefer to say: 'they continued to look like a *church* and be treated like one'. The latter clause is important. It is no use the members of the Church in Wales defining themselves as a 'church' if others do not treat them as one, and the ubiquitous church buildings are powerful visual signs of the Church's inclusive nature. They may also be interpreted, as Davies interprets them, as a sign of its establishment. This is particularly so at a time when economic deprivation in the *outer* cities (Piachaud and Webb 1996, 50; Commission on Social Justice 1994, 323) is leading to the closure of banks and shops in those areas, and when what has been referred to by members of the GB as 'the "Tesco-ization" of the countryside' is leading to the closure of rural post offices and shops. The church building is the last remaining sign that there is anybody 'out there' who cares about these marginalized local communities. Universal provision (such as the National Health Service or the Post Office) is associated with the central state, so universal religious provision does nothing to undermine the traditional assumption that the Church is the state church. Indeed, in urban Wales, forty years after disestablishment, the name many non-churchgoers gave to the Church they did not attend was – 'the Church of England' (Rosser and Harris 1965). At the other end of the social scale, the Church continues to play its traditional role on major state occasions and 'in return' its own major ceremonies continue to be graced by the presence of lords lieutenant and civic dignitaries; and, as Davies notes, the connection between the Church and the Conservative Party persisted in rural areas in the west and north long after the Church's disestablishment and 'did not entirely disappear ... until the 1970s' (Davies 1993, 539).

The Act that threatened to de-church the Welsh Church by disestablishing it not only failed to turn it into a denomination; it was not even fully effective in disestablishing it at the level of popular perception and customary practice. In consequence, even seventy years after its disestablishment, the Church in Wales (its title not withstanding) might more accurately be described as being a 'post-established' church rather than as being, simply and uncomplicatedly, a disestablished one.

There is, however, a further dimension of the dispute over the Church's title that deserves attention. During the hundred years before the invention of the term 'internal colonialism' (Hechter 1975), a similar concept had been current among the advocates of home rule and disestablishment in both Wales and Ireland. Whereas the economic exploitation of the periphery by the central state is essential to the modern connotation of the term, the corresponding nineteenth-century conception was primarily political and religious; economic exploitation was seen in terms of the exploitation of the inhabitants of the periphery not by an alien state but by the members of an alien class resident in the periphery. The Church of Ireland and the Welsh dioceses were therefore not conceived of as the churches of Irish and Welsh Anglicans but as churches whose members were drawn from an expatriate English dominant class. The Welsh dioceses could not be called the Church of Wales, according to this view, because they formed the church not even of a minority of the Welsh but of the English in Wales. The language of the 1914 Act, in referring to the 'church in Wales', while not overtly countenancing this interpretation of the character of the Welsh Church, none the less permits it: for 'church in Wales' read 'the Church of the English (land-owning class) in Wales'. The name 'the Church of Wales' could not be read in this sense. The question arises, therefore, as to whether the interpretation permitted by the wording of the 1914 Act had any basis in fact at the moment of disestablishment.

While there is no adequate evidence such as that which a survey of the membership of the Welsh Church in 1920 would have provided, there can be little doubt that, as far as Wales is concerned, membership of the Anglican Church has never been confined to the expatriate English land-owning class and their dependants. While it is undoubtedly the case that in some parts of Wales characterized by tenant farming the tenants tended to be Welsh Calvinistic Methodists, and the landowners English and Anglican, it is also the case that other rural areas approximated more to the 'English' pattern, with landowners and their employees being Anglican, and dissenting denominations drawing their adherents from artisans and small traders. However, it is in the urban areas of Wales, where by the time of disestablishment the majority of the Welsh population resided, that the assumption of the identity between Anglicanism and English origin and between dissent and Welsh origin is least warranted. The 1851 Census of Religion, taken at what was probably the nadir of Anglican fortunes in Wales, demonstrates that in the urban areas, in spite of the undoubted strength and growth of Nonconformity, adherents of the Church of England (as it then was) remained substantial, Anglicans remaining, in some areas, the most sizeable single religious group. None the less, in the first half of the nineteenth century Anglicanism in Wales suffered so great a loss of adherents to the chapels that it ceased to be the predominant religious group. That is beyond dispute. The point is, rather, that it never has been, even at the lowest point of its fortunes, simply the Church of an expatriate English upper class, even though the members of that class were, of course, adherents of the Church of England.

To deny the charge that the Church had become simply the Church of the English does not, however, dispose of the issue of its relation to Welsh culture. Here the charge has traditionally been that the Church is an alien institution foisted upon the Welsh people by their conquerors. Now it must be freely admitted that this view is clearly itself one of the pieces that make up the mosaic of Welsh culture. The question to be addressed here is whether there was empirical warrant for culturally coding the contemporary Church in Wales as *yr Hen Estrones* (the old stranger) rather than as *yr Hen Fam* (the old mother), a question whose answer is made more difficult by the fact that, historically, it has been coded as both, the emphasis varying across different social groups and different historical epochs.

In considering this question it is somewhat simplistic to define this issue as one of language. It may be pointed out, for example, that the New Testament and the Book of Common Prayer appeared in Welsh in 1567, and that the whole Bible had been translated into Welsh by Bishop William Morgan by 1588. As in the Church of England, the 1960s and 1970s in Wales saw a revision of the forms of worship, and the Church in Wales now has its own prayer book, published in two editions – English only and English and Welsh. The debates of the Church's GB are conducted in both languages, with simultaneous translation of the Welsh for English monoglots. Non-Welsh-speaking bishops have for the last twenty years been the exception rather than the rule, and three out of the four most recent archbishops have had Welsh as their first language.

In spite of this, a European with any familiarity with English culture who attended meetings of the central bodies of the Church would have no doubt that he was witnessing a distinctively English institution. By contrast, observers from the Church of England are struck by the difference between the Church in Wales and their own Church. We observe other cultures necessarily from the standpoint of our own, and their otherness consists in their difference from our own cultural standpoint. There is only one way to do justice to the continental and English perceptions, and that is to recognize that Welsh culture in the sense of the culture of the whole people of Wales is itself a product of the long association between Wales and England. By contrast to the English, the most distinctive characteristic of the Welsh is that they are bicultural, even if the majority of them are not bilingual.

A monocultural English Church in Wales could never claim to be a Church of the Welsh people. By the same token a monocultural Welsh Church could not claim to be the church of the Welsh people either. However any bicultural Church inevitably appears English from the Welsh cultural standpoint, and Welsh from that of England – a situation which approximates to that in which the contemporary Church in Wales finds itself. Being the historic Christian Church in Wales, it is both mother and stranger, having the responsibility of a mother for her children towards the whole people of Wales (Church *of* Wales), to many of whom it has appeared at various times in history as culturally a stranger (Church *in* Wales).

Establishing the necessarily ambivalent character of the Church as a social and cultural institution, as we have attempted to do, says nothing whatever about how, as a matter of fact, the local social groups whose lives are structured by the institution actually behave. At the parish level, it is possible for an institution which is unambiguously a 'church' to behave very much as a 'denomination': that is, for the parish to be a local gathering of its members, whose activities are directed solely to maintaining the life of the group over and against that of the rest of society. The congregations of the Church of England on the Continent are inevitably denominational rather than churchly since the members of the surrounding society have inherited or chosen membership of non-Anglican Christian groups. It is, therefore, quite possible for a Church to be, despite its claims that it is the historic 'church' of a people, *de facto* composed simply of those who denominate themselves as its members. Such a body would be concerned with the provision of a purely pastoral ministry for those members, rather than a group whose *raison d'être* is ministry to the society as a whole.

The likelihood of this being so in the case of the Church in Wales is increased by two factors, one ancient and the other modern. The ancient factor concerns the nineteenth-century predominance of Nonconformity in Wales, and the circumstances surrounding its disestablishment, which must be regarded as highly conducive to the creation of a 'siege mentality'. The modern factor is not peculiar to the Church in Wales. If that Church was at one time an Anglican ark on a sea of Nonconformity and buffeted by political, economic and cultural currents, today all types of religious group find themselves struggling to survive in a social and cultural environment which has, since the 1960s, become rapidly secularized. While such a situation poses problems for all religious groups, notably falling attendances and membership, it poses particular problems for 'churches', since they are, at the normative level, concerned with the spiritual care of the whole population, not just that of their own members. In a highly secularized society this involves the provision of services to those who do not wish to receive them. This problem is evidenced in the Anglican churches of England and Wales by the decline throughout the century in Easter communicants but also, and more recently, by the decline in the number of solemnized marriages, baptisms and even funerals. In the past people have declared their allegiance to a church which they did not regularly attend through their use of what are technically termed its 'occasional offices', which mark key life transitions, and by attendance at major festivals, notably Easter, Christmas and Harvest Festival. The decline in these types of participation by those outside the regular congregation has the effect of closing parishes in on themselves, shifting them from being the local 'church' towards becoming denominational congregations. The inclusive nature of the established Anglican Church has traditionally resulted in Anglican congregations being open to those outside them through the existence of a category of occasional participants. The disestablishment of the Welsh Church in the past, and the secularization of society in the present, therefore pose peculiar problems for it as a religious institution.

It is the role of an established and inclusive Church to 'be there' for the whole population whose Church it is, a population whose members expect and want it to 'be there' for them. Other types of religious group, 'sects' and 'denominations', lack this relation with those outside their congregations and, historically, have seen their evangelistic task as bringing those 'out there' in. However, in Europe as a whole, religious groups have in the past not been in a situation where those 'out there' were pagan or secular. Yet this is the original and apostolic situation of the Christian Church: the apostles (as the Greek term implies) were sent out into the world to preach the Gospel, not to bring people in to an already established social group nor to 'be there' for a sub-Christian population.

The present situation of the Church in Wales is therefore that of a 'post-established' church in a secular society where its churchly character no longer has the consequence that its evangelistic task is necessarily different from that of a denomination or sect: in a secular society all types of Christian religious group are faced with the same primary task of going out from the religious group into a non-religious world to 'preach' the Gospel. However, because the evangelistic imperative applies equally to all branches of Christianity, and because, in a secular society, there is no difference in the nature of that imperative between churches and other types of religious group, it does not follow that the situation of the Church in Wales is the same as that of other religious groups within Wales. It is different, not because

the challenge of the future is different but because the Church in
Wales has a distinctive past. It faces this challenge with resources
and structures that other groups do not have, and as a result has
different opportunities and difficulties arising therefrom.

THE CHURCH IN WALES AT THE BEGINNING
OF THE NINETIES

The most distinctive feature of the Church is its territorial organization, which is the historic organization of the English Church
in which a province (such as Canterbury or York) led by an archbishop comprises a number of dioceses, each under the authority
of a bishop. The dioceses are in turn divided into archdeaconries
(areas of jurisdiction of archdeacons), and the archdeaconries
into deaneries. A deanery (traditionally termed a 'rural deanery'
whether its area is rural or not) is a grouping of parishes led by a
'rural dean'. Parishes are served by parish priests. Each office in
the hierarchy is associated therefore with a particular territory,
and the hierarchy is based on the size of the territory for which
the officer is responsible. In Wales, however, the highest office,
that of archbishop (or 'metropolitan'), is not at present associated
with any particular diocese. The archbishop, who is elected from
among the bishops, is simultaneously bishop of his diocese and
Archbishop of Wales, and his seat is in the cathedral of the
diocese of which he is bishop. In other words no diocese is
defined as the metropolitical see, though this situation has
recently been under review.

This traditional organizational form comprises two distinct
elements. The first stems from the historic form of Christian
ministry in which there are three orders of minister: bishops,
priests and deacons. The central function of bishops is 'apostolic'. Like the original apostles, bishops are both persons who
are sent and persons who send. They are ministers authorized
and sent by the Church out into the world to preach the Gospel
and to celebrate the sacraments within the household (*oikos*) of
faith which they established, who in turn authorized other ministers to preach the Gospel and celebrate the sacraments and sent
them to places which were outside that household (*para-oikos*, i.e.
to 'parishes'). The strategic site of the initial household of faith

within an area was normally a 'town' in the sense of a 'central place': that is, a settlement which was the economic and political centre of its surrounding area. The responsibility for the outlying places was therefore shared between the sender and the sent, between the bishop and his priests, who came to be known in England as 'vicars' who shared with the bishop the 'cure of souls' in their parishes.

The second element of the traditional territorial organization of the Church is administrative: that is, pragmatic rather than normative in origin. With the establishment of Christianity as the dominant religion of an area, the function of church organization ceased to be that of sending (*apostole*) and proclamation (*kerygma*) and became, rather, that of faithful witness (*martyria*) to a traditional (i.e. handed-down) faith. A town and its hinterland, a bishop and his priests, became an area of ecclesiastical administration which took the Latin name for such an area, *diocese*. Bishops came to be assisted in the oversight (*episcope*) of their dioceses by archdeacons, and where there was more than one archdeacon each had responsibility for a part of a diocese (archdeaconry). The deanery is, by contrast, not part of the 'central administration' of a diocese but a grouping of contiguous parishes and their clergy under the chairmanship of one of them ('the rural dean') which makes possible local co-operation between parishes and is a means of communication between the parishes constituting it and the diocese.

The appropriateness to Wales of this form of organization, which has its origins in Roman times, is questionable since, throughout most of its history, Wales has not been made up of towns and their hinterlands, thus posing problems for the newly disestablished Church when it became responsible for its own territorial organization. This issue is discussed in more detail in Chapter 3.

The area under the ecclesiastical jurisdiction of the Church in Wales is virtually identical with that of the Principality. (It is not completely identical, since some Welsh parishes bordering England were permitted to opt out of the new province at disestablishment and remained part of the Church of England.) It comprises six dioceses. The four original dioceses at the time of disestablishment (Bangor, St Asaph, St Davids and Llandaff), originated in the sixth century, corresponded to the ancient Welsh kingdoms of Gwynedd, Powys, Deheubarth and Morgannwg, and are associated with St Deiniol, St Kentigern, St David and St Teilo respectively. After disestablishment, two new dioceses were created. The present diocese of Monmouth was created in 1921 out of the original diocese of Llandaff, and the present diocese of Swansea and Brecon was created in 1923 out of the original diocese of St Davids.

There are at present fourteen archdeaconries in the province, the dioceses of St Asaph and St Davids each having three archdeaconries, and each of the other dioceses two. In 1989 the Province comprised seventy-seven rural deaneries. The average size of a deanery was 7.8 benefices, ranging from 4.5 in the archdeaconry of Merioneth to 10.5 in the archdeaconry of Margam.

A benefice is a territorial unit in the care of a single priest. It may be a 'single' parish or comprise several parishes. In the latter case it is termed a 'group benefice'. By 1959 the grouping of parishes had reduced the number of benefices to 884. In 1989 there were 1,134 parishes in the Church in Wales, but the number of benefices had fallen to 604, a fall over the previous thirty years of 32 per cent. Over the same period the number of parochial clergy fell from 1,341 to 690, a fall of 49 per cent, and the ratio of clergy to benefices fell from 1.52 to 1.14. In 1989 the average population of a benefice was 4,757 and the average population of a parish was 2,533.

The territorial organization of the Church involves the division of its territory into a set of areas which are both exclusive (i.e. not overlapping) and exhaustive (every part of the territory is covered). This form of organization is clearly that of an inclusive church rather than that of a denomination or sect. Similarly, the population size of the units involved is relatively small and would be even smaller were it not for the grouping of parishes.

The necessity for the grouping of parishes reflects, however, the difficulties involved in trying to maintain a traditional, 'established church', organizational stance in a non-traditional (i.e. secular) society. The reasons for the grouping of parishes are many, and several reasons frequently operate in the same case. Two distinct causes may be distinguished, however: lack of viability and lack of clergy. Where the first cause operates it will involve the grouping of parishes too small to support themselves in terms of their income and attendance. Such conditions are likely to arise owing to the sparsity of population or to a low proportion of Anglican membership in a given population, or to both. Such parishes will be termed 'non-viable', and benefices comprising such parishes 'non-viable' groupings. However, some benefices are made up of viable parishes. Here the motive for grouping would appear to be the scarcity of resources. In 1989 half of the group benefices were groupings of viable parishes. The two causes are, of course, interrelated. Areas with small populations are generally also areas of low density. Maintaining exhaustive geographical coverage in areas of low population density involves the grouping of non-viable parishes which, even after grouping, are still of low densities and high clergy-to-people ratios. This represents a drain on the resources for clergy payment and reduces the overall amount of money available for the payment of clergy in viable parishes, which in turn increases the extent of the grouping of such parishes.

The Church in Wales finds itself in this position because it has central funds which can be used for the payment of clergy. In 1992 its income was £16.8 million of which 74 per cent was spent on clergy pensions and stipends. If, as is the case in many other religious organizations, each local church had to pay the major part of the cost of its minister, then non-viable parishes would have no clergy, since in low-density areas the number of parishes whose grouping was required to support a parish priest would constitute an area of so great an extent that it could not be served by one person.

Oscar Wilde remarked after two decades of agricultural depression in the nineteenth century that 'land provides you with social position but deprives you of the means of keeping it up'. He should, of course, have said 'does not provide you with *sufficient* means to keep it up'. The Church in Wales has inherited an establishment tradition of exhaustive territorial coverage and universal provision, but re-endowment and subsequent efforts to raise capital have not provided it with means of keeping it up which are sufficient in a secular society where falling membership reduces the total contributions made by local church members to the Church, unless their *per capita* giving in real terms becomes very substantially greater than it was at the beginning of the century, and more than the 1996 figure of £3.65 per week per attender.

Defining the 'target population' of the Church as those claiming membership of it plus those not claiming membership of any religious denomination, the target population is 82 per cent of the Welsh population (Brierley 1983) or roughly 3,800 persons per benefice in 1989. These figures must be compared with the Church's actual membership. Membership is notoriously difficult to measure in the case of religious groups. Since 1990 the Church in Wales has published statistics for six types of participation: communicants (at Christmas, Easter, Pentecost (Whitsun) and the third Sunday after Trinity), numbers on the electoral roll, and a measure of average Sunday attendance. We shall be considering these 'official statistics' and the changes in them since 1990 in the last part of this chapter. We shall use the official 1990 figures for Easter communicants (ECs) and the 1989 survey figures for 'average communicants'. This last is a measure of *congregational size* and averages two observations: the number communicating on Advent Sunday (four weeks before Christmas) and on Trinity Sunday (the Sunday after Whitsun).

The average congregational size in 1989 was seventy-five – about 2 per cent of the target population. Of these an average of eighteen held some office or were responsible for some activity. By subtracting the average congregational size from the average EC figure, we find that in the average benefice there are 116 other people who attend occasionally. The total average lay membership is, therefore, 191 or 5.0 per cent of the target population. (The official figures for 1990 put the total lay membership slightly lower and the average attendance figure slightly higher than the 1989 survey estimate.) There is one church for every 28.7 members of a congregation, for every seventy-two ECs and for approximately every 1,500 of the target population. The average benefice had an income of around £25,000 in 1990.

So far we have considered provincial averages. If these are replaced by totals, we can arrive at the following description of the Church in Wales on the basis of the 1989 survey, and the official figures for 1990 where more reliable. The Church had 108,000 ECs (1990), or 4.6 per cent of the Welsh population over the age of fourteen. Its weekly communicants totalled 45,750 (1989), or just under 2 per cent of the Welsh population over the age of fourteen. Its attendances totalled 62,850 (1990), or 2.2 per cent of the total population of Wales.

These figures do not suggest a great dissimilarity between the Church in Wales and the Church of England, since the Church of England figures for 1989 show ECs as forming 3.5 per cent and Sunday communicants as forming just under 2 per cent of the population over the age of fourteen, and attendances as forming 2.4 per cent of the total population (Church of England Central Board of Finance 1997). The only significant difference between the English and Welsh figures is in the proportion formed by ECs of the population over fourteen, which was higher in Wales than in England.

At the beginning of the decade the Church had 881 active clergy, over 10,000 'lay workers', 763 church halls (1989) and 1,593 churches (1990). The benefices between them had a total income of £15.5 million, and spent £14.9 million. The RB made contributions towards the cost of stipends and housing and paid the whole cost of clergy pensions, its total contribution amounting to £12.2 million, or 72 per cent of the total cost of the ministry (1990). The total cost of maintaining the existing pastoral structure of the Church in 1990 therefore amounted to £27.1 million, or approximately £45,000 a benefice, of which the average benefice raised about half.

If we focus on the Church as an organization (rather than on its relation to its environment), this bald statistical picture would seem to be one of an organization which is well-resourced in terms of plant, income and active members and is by virtue of its territorial organization highly pervasive. Indeed, many secular voluntary organizations would be delighted to have so many resources and such a comprehensive and well-staffed territorial organization. If, however, we focus on the relation between organization and environment, the picture is much changed. Church membership amounts to a tiny proportion of the population, a circumstance that cannot any longer be explained away by the adherence of large numbers of the Welsh to other religious groups, since surveys of the Welsh population (Brierley 1983) have indicated that those participating in non-Anglican religious groups constitute only a small proportion of the total population, the rest of which the 'post-established' Church must regard as its responsibility.

The figures make clear the extent to which the Church can only maintain its comprehensive coverage as a result of its central

funds. Even then the funds available for the running of a benefice
are scarcely adequate to maintain it. The superabundance of
plant is not an unmixed blessing, since the buildings concerned,
though frequently beautiful, are, even more frequently, very old,
costly to maintain and heat, and quite often (because of the
movement of population in the last five hundred or so years) in
the 'wrong' place. The territorial organization of the Church and
its associated buildings, instead of being a springboard from
which the Church can evangelize the world, is, rather, a sponge
which absorbs time, energy and money in its maintenance.
Energy and money are not, however, discrete entities. A great
deal of energy may be absorbed in raising money to maintain the
ministry and the plant. The net result may be the 'denomina-
tionalizing' of the congregation: its transformation into a group of
individuals who denominate themselves as Anglicans and who
band together to provide services for their members rather than
orientating themselves to the society of which they claim to be the
Church.

It was the situation outlined above, which we have described as
that of a post-establishment church in a secular society, that
formed the context of the Church's responses to the call of the
last Lambeth Conference to the Anglican Communion to make
the 1990s a 'decade of evangelism'. One of those responses was
to ask the authors of the present study to collect the data that
form the basis of the following chapters and to make reports to
the GB so that the whole Church might consider its situation and
come to its own judgement on the 'State of the Church'.

The Church in a secular society

What that enquiry was not required to do, however, was to
consider the issue of 'secularization'. There is an enormous sociological literature on this topic, both theoretical and empirical,
and the issue of secularization became in the early nineties a
subject of controversy among sociologists of religion. The reasons
for this are straightforward. Sociological writing in the nineteenth
century and the first half of the twentieth tended to operate
against a set of background assumptions to the effect that
contemporary societies were undergoing a process of change
('modernization') which involved the inevitable decline of reli-

gious belief and practice. At the same time there was also a view which held that religion (or something very like it) was a functional necessity for any society. Faced with the incontrovertible facts of the decline of participation in mainstream, conventional religion since World War II, those holding this theoretical position naturally became interested in exploring non-conventional forms of religion.

At the same time the legitimacy of the traditional secularization theory was weakened by the sociological loss of faith in the existence of an inevitable modernization process, by public disenchantment with science and by the appearance of an increasing number of quasi-religious movements, many of a sectarian nature. To this was added, in the last fifteen years, the re-emergence of religious belief in the countries once constituting the Soviet Union and in its satellites, the resurgence of Islam and the development of, at least nominally, religious strife in the former Yugoslavia, not to mention its continuance in Northern Ireland. It therefore became increasingly difficult to maintain that religion was an outmoded and dying form of social practice having little relevance to the contemporary world. In short, recent decades have produced ample evidence of major religious change but made it very hard, in the absence of any measure of religiosity which could be made of whole populations, to arrive at any clear view as to whether these changes amounted to an overall decline.

It is important, however, to remember that the root sociological meaning of 'secularization' is not something that is experienced by religious groups but something that happens to society. Its core meaning is the separation within society of religious institutions from other social institutions, and of religious knowledge from other forms of knowledge. This is relatively uncontroversial. The second meaning of secularization is given by its reference to an allegedly observed trend in modern (i.e. urban-industrial) societies for religious belief and practice to decline. The third meaning refers, primarily, not to institutions or behaviour but to culture. The secularization of culture is regarded as an established fact, as far as European societies are concerned, and is then referred to in order to explain observations of decline in participation in traditional religious institutions and practices.

It seems to us incontrovertible that Christianity in Britain has, in the last half-century, lost its cultural hegemony. We cannot argue this in detail here but can provide an instance of the loss: religious news is no longer routinely reported in BBC Radio 4 news bulletins but is confined to a religious ghetto between 7.30 and 9 on Sunday mornings. This may be contrasted with sport, which, although it has its own weekend slot on Saturday mornings, figures prominently in main BBC newscasts and magazine programmes.

In the introduction to his superb lectures *The Secularization of the European Mind in the Nineteenth Century*, Owen Chadwick remarks: 'the [historical] problem of secularization is not the same as the problem of the Enlightenment. Enlightenment was of the few. Secularization was of the many' (Chadwick 1990, 9). The view that the decline in participation in mainstream religion in the twentieth century can be explained by the secularization of culture can be interpreted as the claim that it is to be explained by reference to the 'culture of the few', and involves the assumption that this then 'trickles down' to influence the 'culture of the many'. Chadwick will have none of this, favouring (because he is concerned with secularization rather than the Enlightenment) the approach of social historians who are 'little interested in intellectual elites until their conclusions are seized upon by a society which is ready to seize upon them' (1990, 9).

What Chadwick's study describes, therefore, is the result of change not just in 'high' culture but in culture in the anthropological sense as the way of life of a whole people. The adoption of secular modes of thought so that they become prevalent throughout the whole society requires explanation by reference to circumstances other than those modes of thought alone. The emergence of secular modes of thought cannot, therefore, be used to explain, by itself, the loss of the hegemony of Christian belief, and hence cannot satisfactorily explain the decline in participation in mainstream religion to which we now turn.

Wales may be a special case, but it is a special case of something more general occurring throughout Britain which provides a context within which to understand that case. Bruce (1995a) has recently brought together a number of statistics describing religious change in this century, many of them based on the work of Brierley of MARC Europe, chiefly his *Century of British Christianity* (Brierley 1985).

First there is the decline in membership of the Christian churches in Britain, which fell between 1900 and 1990 from 30 to 12 per cent of the adult population, the sharpest fall being experienced in the period after 1950, especially 1970–90. In other words, membership measured in these terms was only 40 per cent of what it had been in 1900. The comparable figure for the Church of England was even lower – only 29 per cent – the Church's membership having fallen by 1990 to 55 per cent of its 1900 level. Due to net immigration and higher fertility, Roman Catholic membership rose over the same period to 225 per cent of its 1900 level. However, even Catholic membership ceased to grow after 1970.

When we turn to attendances, however, the Roman Catholic position is much less advantageous, since the proportion of members attending mass fell between 1900 and 1990 from 80 to 40 per cent. The number of Catholics attending Mass in 1990 was only 38 per cent higher than at the beginning of the period, and these figures mask the fact that the 1990 attendances were 20 per cent down on those of 1970. If we consider adult attendances at Christian churches in Britain in a broader historical perspective, we find that these fell from 50 per cent of the adult population of England and Wales in 1851 to 20 per cent in 1960, and to just under 10 per cent in 1990. Indeed, the decline in attendances, as a proportion of the adult population, has been running at an annual rate which was twice as high in the period 1960–90 as in the period 1851–1960.

Do these figures show that, by the 1990s, Britain had become a secular society? They have certainly led many observers, such as Bruce (1995b), to claim support from the British data for the secularization thesis in its 'observed trend form' – despite data such as those provided by the 1991 British Social Attitudes Survey (Jowell et al. 1992, 294) that a quarter of the population of Britain has a strong faith, and another quarter a rather weaker faith, in the existence of God. We do not propose to enter this debate here, but merely observe that all the British mainstream churches appear to be experiencing decline in one form or another (Davie 1994, 49).

If we look in more detail at recent Church of England figures, we find that, between 1970 and 1990, ECs (as percentages of population over the age of fourteen) have fallen by an amount equivalent to 24 per cent, attendances (as a percentage of total population) by 27 per cent, baptisms (as a percentage of live births) by an amount equivalent to 41 per cent, and confirmations by 47 per cent (Church of England Central Board of Finance 1997). There is no hiding the fact that falls of this magnitude over twenty years, especially the falls in baptisms and confirmations, must put the future of the Church of England, at least in its present form, in question, coming as they do on top of the steady decline between 1900 and 1970.

No comparable figures are available for the Church in Wales except in respect of ECs. The Church's ECs have declined from 7.4 per cent of the population over the age of fourteen in 1970, to 4.6 per cent in 1990, a fall of the magnitude of 38 per cent and thus greater than that experienced by the Church of England. Between 1990 and 1995 Church of England ECs as a proportion of the population over fourteen declined by a further 6.2 per cent of their 1970 level. In the Church in Wales the fall was equivalent to 8.4 per cent of their 1970 level. In England in 1995, ECs formed 3.2 per cent of the population over fourteen; in Wales, they formed 4.0 per cent. The last figures suggest that Wales is still 'behind' England on this measure of secularization, therefore, but the earlier figures show it is 'catching up' fast. Other official figures for the quinquennium show that the Church in Wales is suffering the same rapid decline as the Church of England. Attendances as a percentage of total population fell in the five years from 2.3 to 1.8 (Church of England, 2.4 to 2.1). Calculating falls as a percentage of 1990 numbers, baptisms fell by 21 per cent (Church of England, 18 per cent), confirmations by 30 per cent (Church of England, 27 per cent) and weddings by 31 per cent (Church of England, not available).

Is there, then, aught for the Church's comfort? There are two encouraging signs. One is that direct personal giving has risen by 72 per cent from £2.12 to £3.65 per week over the first six years of the decade; the other is that the share of the cost of the ministry borne by the Church's RB has fallen from 71.9 per cent in 1990 to 67.4 per cent in 1995. In other words, remaining church members and attenders show signs of greater commitment and financial responsibility. Unfortunately for the Church as *ecclesia*, this may well also be interpreted as a sign of the Church's gradual 'denominalization'. It is likely that people are willing to pay more towards the cost of their church to maintain the services that it provides to *them*. If this is the motivation behind the giving, it bodes ill for the future of a religious body dedicated to the service of one who is, *par excellence*, a 'man for *others*'.

This work is, then, a study of a post-establishment church in a secular society. The problems confronted in being a 'church' in such a society are of two major kinds. The first are connected with the church as an organization which has a territorial structure, and the first part of this book involves the description and analysis of the territorial units which made up the Church in Wales at the beginning of the nineties (Chapters 2–4). The second part of the book is concerned primarily with the people who inhabit the units making up the structure and with the relation between their location in that structure and their attitudes towards their environments, both ecclesiastical and secular. The final chapters reflect on the conclusions of earlier chapters and attempt to understand them by moving beyond a characterization of contemporary society merely as 'secular'.

Part One

Territorial organization and resource distribution

2

Describing a territorial organization

The data upon which the first part of this book is based derive from a survey of the benefices of the Church in Wales – a survey, that is to say, of the territorial units that constitute it. Unlike most social surveys, the units surveyed were not people but parishes, since a benefice is a geographical area in the charge of one ordained person (a cleric), and such an area is either a parish or a group of parishes. At the time of the survey carried out in 1989, the Church in Wales contained 604 benefices, and responses were received from 549 of them, the remaining benefices being vacant. In order to use the characteristics of benefices to describe the Church, it was necessary to classify them according to their key characteristics and thereby establish benefice 'types'. The establishment of these types made possible a description of the Church's dioceses in terms of the distribution of the benefices in each diocese over the categories of each type, and over other characteristics not included in the type. (This description is provided in Chapter 3.) It also made possible the investigation of the *relationships* between different types and characteristics. (This is the task of Chapter 4.) The primary task of this chapter is to describe the Church in terms of the distribution of its benefices over these types and other important characteristics. However, initially the way the types were constructed is explained briefly, because the attempt to construct benefice types itself reveals important characteristics of the benefices of the Church in Wales.

Many distributions approximate the shape of a normal curve, being roughly symmetrical, with a majority of units having values which are in the middle of the range, and minorities having very high or very low values. That is the way in which most people think, however unfamiliar the terminology. So most parishioners think that their parish is 'normal', in the sense of typical, with small minorities of untypical parishes on either side of it. For example, small benefices with low parochial incomes, and large benefices with high incomes, would be held to constitute atypical minorities on either side of the majority of parishes of medium size and income 'like ours'. In fact, not only is the range over which benefices are distributed on key characteristics very wide; they also do not cluster in the middle of these ranges. Congregational size and benefice income (for example) have distributions in which benefices cluster at the lower end (small size and low income), a cluster which is balanced by a very wide distribution of the remainder over higher sizes and incomes. Such markedly non-normal distributions cannot adequately be described by way of averages, and policies directed towards the average benefice inevitably fail because they 'fit' very few benefices. 'Average' statistics, such as those quoted in the previous chapter, do not reflect the situation of the majority of parishes and therefore provide only the most preliminary understanding of the reality they purport to describe. The example given illustrates the problems faced by a Church which serves an area containing a wide range of settlement types and which therefore has the twin tasks of maintaining services to rural areas with small dispersed populations and struggling to evangelize large secular urban populations.

Characteristics of benefices

In the analysis that follows, benefices are described in terms of three different types of characteristics: *secular, administrative* and *pastoral*. Since benefices vary in many ways, it proves valuable for certain purposes to work with a small number of strategically important derived variables. Within the secular and the administrative sphere respectively the *secular type* and the *ecclesiastical classification* were each constructed by combining simple benefice characteristics, and they constitute the chief ways in which benefices were classified. The third major characteristic, *benefice type,* is relevant to both the secular and the administratve (ecclesiastical) spheres, since it arises from the administrative practice of grouping parishes in response to their secular characteristics (such as sparsity of population). At this stage it may be helpful to summarize the attributes and derived variables that enter into the account and that are also referred to in the two following chapters.

The area and the population of a benefice are basic secular variables, and from these the density of its population may be derived. A combination of population size and density is used to construct the key variable in this category, *secular type*, which also concerns position on the urban–rural continuum.

The administrative characteristics of a benefice may be roughly grouped to take in (a) considerations of resources and (b) aspects of its structure. Under (a) the attempt was made to determine the extent to which a benefice was relatively 'advantaged' or 'disadvantaged' in terms of its resources. The basic variables of congregational size and benefice income are highly indicative in this respect. However, the numbers of clergy associated with a benefice, and also the number of parishes of which it is composed, have major resource implications. A combination of these variables was used to construct the important *ecclesiastical classification*, centrally concerned with relative advantage or disadvantage. The number of open churches within a benefice is also picked out as a variable with major administrative implications. Benefices may be further differentiated in respect of how they acquire and how they spend funds. Two key variables considered subsequently, but not in this chapter, are the percentage of income derived from collections and the percentage of overall expenditure devoted to the diocesan quota. The structure of benefices (b) may take various forms. The main distinctions concern whether they consist of single parishes or of groups of parishes, and whether or not those parishes are viable. This leads to a classification in terms of *benefice type*. Though dealt with here as an administrative characteristic, this characteristic has important links to the secular sphere, as noted above.

A number of basic and derived variables may be broadly distinguished from those considered so far and classified as pastoral characteristics. In a Welsh context, benefices may be distinguished in respect of the language(s) used in services. One may also attempt to develop indicators of the extent of membership within a benefice and the number of active participants in parish life. Among the more important derived ratios are the proportion of the total population formed by all members, the proportion of all members who are practising, and the proportion of practising members who are active (in the sense of holding an office or having a sphere of responsibility). The proportion that confirmations form of baptisms was also calculated.

The three different types of characteristics are set out below.

Secular characteristics
population size
density of population
secular type (size and density)

Administrative characteristics
congregational size
benefice income
number of parishes
number of clergy in benefice
ecclesiastical classification
number of open churches
% of income from collections
% of expenditure on diocesan quota
benefice type (groups; viability)

Pastoral characteristics
language used in services
number of Easter
    communicants (ECs)
active participants in parish
    ('lay workers')
proportion ECs form of
    population
proportion of all members
    practising
proportion of practising
    members active
ratio of confirmations to
    baptisms

Secular characteristics: secular type

The survey provided two pieces of information concerning purely secular characteristics of each benefice: the size of its population and its area. Benefice populations ranged in size from below 850 (the 10 per cent of benefices with the smallest populations) to over 12,400 (the 10 per cent of benefices with the largest populations). Areas also ranged enormously from below 307 hectares (the 10 per cent of benefices with the smallest areas) to above 8,238 hectares (the 10 per cent with the largest areas). However, what matters from the point of view of pastoral provision is not so much area as population size and the density of population. Benefice densities ranged from below 0.15 persons per hectare in the lowest 10 per cent of benefices to over 13 persons per hectare in the highest 10 per cent.

The pastoral and evangelistic challenge faced by benefices will vary with both population size and density. Benefices which may be considered advantaged by virtue of their small size (having a high clergy-to-people ratio) may be considered disadvantaged if their small size is combined with low density, which will involve considerable travelling on the part of the incumbent. The two measures, size and density, were therefore combined to create a range of *secular types*. This was done by dividing the distributions of benefices over size and over density each into three equal parts, the top third being classified as high, the middle third as medium, and the bottom third as low. These two classifications were then combined to create a range of types in respect of population size and density which may be thought of as providing a scale whose points lie on the urban–rural continuum. This range, together with the associated distribution of benefices, is set out in Table 2.1.

Table 2.1   **The distribution of benefices by *secular type***

Size	Density	Secular type	Number	%
high	high	city	128	23.5
medium	high	large town	35	6.4
high	medium	urban aggregation	40	7.4
high	low		0	0.0
low	high		1[*]	0.2
medium	medium	large rural nucleated	138	25.4
low	medium	small rural nucleated	40	7.4
medium	low	large rural dispersed	39	7.2
low	low	small rural dispersed	123	22.6
ALL			544	100.1

[*]This benefice has been included in the 'large rural nucleated' category for subsequent purposes. Five benefices failed to provide sufficient information to be classified.

It will be seen that, combining size and density, we do not get an approximately normal distribution with most benefices in the middle, and minorities in the urban and rural extremes. On the contrary, 72 per cent of benefices divide approximately equally between the categories 'city' (urban: large size, high density), 'large rural nucleated' (rural: medium size, medium density) and 'small rural dispersed' (rural: small size, low density). An urban benefice has a population of over 6,000, a middling benefice one of between 2,000 and 6,000, and a rural benefice one of under 2,000. An urban benefice has a density in excess of 5.53 persons per hectare, a middling benefice one of between 0.42 and 5.53, and a rural benefice one of below 0.42 persons per hectare. In terms of the 1974 local authority districts, the contrast is between Merioneth (rural), Llanelli and Port Talbot (middling) and Torfaen, Newport, Swansea and Cardiff (urban).

The usefulness of the classification in terms of secular type was then tested by determining whether it was significantly correlated with each of all the other survey variables. A significant relation was found in 61 per cent of cases.

Administrative characteristics: the ecclesiastical classification

In respect of the administrative sphere, two primary ways of classifying benefices were developed. The *ecclesiastical classification* centred on how advantaged or disadvantaged the benefice was in terms of its human and material resources. Of particular importance in this connection are congregational size and benefice income. The other primary mode of classification is *benefice type* (see below), which has to do with the extent of grouping of parishes and the issue of their viability.

Congregational size
Obviously it is impossible to have a very large congregation in a benefice whose population is very small. None the less, at higher population sizes it is possible for there to be wide variation in the size of a congregation among benefices of the same population size. It is legitimate, therefore, to regard congregational size as partially independent of population size and as being primarily a characteristic of the Church rather than of the local community. As indicated above, congregational size was measured by averaging the communicants on two selected Sundays. The median point of the distribution (the size which marked the boundary between the upper half and the lower half of the distribution) was sixty. Benefices were classified as having 'small' or 'large' congregations according to whether these numbered below or above sixty.

Benefice income
While congregational size must affect the size of a benefice's income, income is more powerfully affected by the wealth of the members of its congregation. Benefice income can therefore be

regarded as a characteristic of the congregation which is partially independent of the secular variables of population size and density, and can be regarded for the purposes of the analysis of the data provided by the survey as an ecclesiastical, not a secular, characteristic. Benefice income ranged from below £7,380 (the lowest 10 per cent of benefices) to above £42,010 per annum (the highest 10 per cent). The lowest benefice income recorded was £1,280, and there were three benefices with incomes of over £100,000. The income that marked the border between the upper and lower halves of the distribution was £16,000. Benefices were classified as 'rich' if they had incomes of above £16,000, and as 'poor' if they were below that figure.

The two characteristics, congregational size and benefice income, were then cross-tabulated to form the basis of the ecclesiastical classification. This basic classification was then modified by the addition of two further characteristics.

Number of clergy and number of parishes
'Large, rich' benefices were distinguished according to whether or not they had one or more parochial clergy. 'Small poor' benefices were distinguished according to whether they comprised merely one or two parishes, as opposed to three or more. These discriminations increased the number of categories in the classification from four to six. The distribution of benefices over these six categories is shown in Table 2.2. The usefulness of the ecclesiastical classification was then tested by determining the proportion of all the other survey variables with which it was significantly correlated. A significant relationship was found in 60 per cent of cases. The *ecclesiastical classification* is unambiguously a scale of 'resource advantage' (people and money), by contrast to the *secular type*, which classifies benefices according to how urban or rural are the settlements in which they are situated.

It has been seen in our discussion of the *secular type* that 72 per cent of benefices were concentrated in only three of its nine categories. It will be seen from Table 2.2 that the *ecclesiastical classification* shows an uneven distribution on the scale of advantage, the largest categories on the two primary criteria being 'large, rich' and 'small, poor' which between them accounted for 76 per cent of all benefices. Again, nearly two-fifths of 'large, rich' benefices had two or more clergy, while at the other end of

Table 2.2   The distribution of benefices according to the
ecclesiastical classification **(scale of relative resource advantage)**

Congregational size	Benefice income	Further structural feature	Number	%
'large'	'rich'	clergy: 2 or more	80	14.9
'large'	'rich'	clergy: 1	125	23.3
'large'	'poor'	none	67	12.5
'small'	'rich'	none	64	11.9
'small'	'poor'	parishes: 1 or 2	140	26.1
'small'	'poor'	parishes: 3 or more	61	11.4
TOTAL			537	100.1

Twelve benefices failed to provide sufficient information to be classified.

the scale just under one-third of 'small, poor' benefices comprised three or more parishes. The most frequently found types were 'large, rich' benefices with one cleric, and 'small, poor' benefices comprising not more than two parishes.

Administrative characteristics: number of parishes and churches

Only a minority of all benefices (45 per cent) were single-parish benefices; 29 per cent of benefices comprised only two parishes, 15 per cent three parishes and the remainder (11 per cent) were groups of parishes numbering between four and seven. As would be expected given the amalgamation of parishes, it was not the case that the most frequently found kind of benefice was one with a single church. Only approximately one-fifth of all benefices had just one church, a third of all benefices had two. A substantial minority (a quarter) had three churches, and 16 per cent four; the remaining benefices ranged between five and seven. Three-quarters of the benefices held a weekly service in each of their churches. On the other hand, 16 per cent did not hold a weekly service in at least one of their churches. Out of the 1,453 churches belonging to the responding parishes, only 243 (17 per cent) did not have at least a weekly service, though 407 churches (28 per cent), located in one-third of the benefices, had no weekly Communion service. The difference between the

proportion of churches with no weekly service and the proportion
of those with no weekly Communion service indicates the extent
to which maintenance of services in multi-church benefices is
dependent on the use of lay readers.

Administrative characteristics: benefice type

Benefices varied according to their formal composition and the
viability of their components. Traditionally a parochial benefice
was a single parish. At the time of the survey, however, over 55
per cent of all benefices were made up of more than one parish.
A tiny proportion of these are 'rectorial benefices': one unit
comprising several erstwhile parishes for which a single cleric
with the title of rector is responsible to the bishop. The rector is
assisted by a staff of clergy. This arrangement makes it possible
for a set of contiguous parishes to be run by a group of clergy and
gives scope for a variety of forms of the organization of ministry
within it.

The majority of benefices comprising several parishes are,
however, 'group benefices' which have come about not through
positive policy but as expedient responses to declining populations, lack of appropriate priests, lack of financial resources, or
any combination of these factors. In order to distinguish group
benefices whose parishes had been grouped because they were no
longer viable on their own from those which had been grouped
owing to lack of resources, parishes within group benefices were
assessed as to their viability, and each group benefice then classified according to the viability of the parishes that composed it.
The criteria for viability adopted in this study were that a parish
should have no fewer than 50 ECs and an annual income of not
less than £5,000. A group benefice was classified as a group of
non-viable parishes if the average income and the communicant
numbers of the component parishes failed to meet both these
criteria.

It transpired that of the 549 benefices surveyed 3 per cent were
rectorial benefices, while 45 per cent were single parishes; of the
rest, 26 per cent were groups of viable parishes and a further 26
per cent groups of non-viable parishes. It follows that, while the
category into which benefices most frequently fall is that of
the single parish where the benefice has the traditional 'one

incumbent, one parish' structure, these traditional benefices are none the less in a minority: over half the benefices are the result of grouping. Moreover, half of these group benefices are made up of non-viable parishes. The parishes in this type of benefice should, on purely administrative criteria, have been 'united' to form a single parish; they should be found, that is to say, in the 'single-parish' category. By contrast, the existence of groups of viable parishes reflects the shortage of 'appropriate' (e.g. 'Welsh-speaking') clergy and/or money.

The ecclesiastical classification and benefice type

It should be noted that the term 'viability' does not refer to the viability of a benefice but to the viability of the parishes that compose it. In consequence it does not follow that all group benefices composed of 'non-viable' parishes fall into the 'small, poor' category of the ecclesiastical classification. There is, of course, a relation between the two classifications. First, the proportion of grouped benefices comprising *non-viable* parishes rises from 9 per cent among 'large, rich'-grouped benefices to 81 per cent of 'small, poor'-grouped benefices. Benefices composed of 'non-viable' parishes are found most frequently (40 per cent) among benefices classified as 'small, poor, with three or more parishes'. The remainder are distributed equally over the remaining categories of the ecclesiasical classification. It has to be recognized, however, that as a result of grouping, a set even of non-viable parishes can form a benefice classified in the 'large, rich' category. In fact 6 per cent of benefices made up of non-viable parishes are of this type. Secondly, the proportion of group benefices rises from 20 per cent among the 'large, rich' benefices with more than one cleric to 59 per cent among 'small, poor' benefices. This last figure includes fifty-nine benefices that were still classified as 'non-viable' in terms of size and income in spite of the fact that they contained three or more parishes. It follows from these considerations that the relationship between the two variables is complex and that *benefice type* is interdependent with the structural element of the *ecclesiastical classification* rather than being an independent variable in its own right. The key point is that a scale of relative advantage (the ecclesiastical classification) necessarily focuses on resource input, but the degree of advantage depends also upon the structure of the entity (benefice type) that the resources are required to sustain.

Pastoral characteristics

Language

One of the problems faced by the Church in Wales derives not from the fact that the population to which it ministers is bilingual but from the fact that its population is composed of two linguistic groups one of which is bilingual (Welsh and English) and the other monolingual (English only). The official policy of the Church has been to promote the use of the Welsh language in its meetings and services. Ordinands are encouraged to acquire a competence in the Welsh language, and such competence, while not a prerequisite, is an advantage in clergy career advancement, if only because it widens the range of benefices that a priest can serve. The Church is, however, hindered in its pursuit of bilingualism – and even in its provision of Welsh-speaking clergy to Welsh-speaking benefices – by the demographics of Welsh speaking in Wales. While a large part of the geographical *area* covered by the Church has a substantial proportion of Welsh speakers, the majority of the *population* resides in areas which are predominantly English-speaking. The proportion of ordinands who speak Welsh reflects the relatively low proportion of Welsh speakers in the population. The proportion of benefices which have to be served by Welsh-speaking clergy reflects the relative size of those parts of Wales with high proportions of Welsh-speaking people, thus creating a mismatch between the linguistic competence of clergy and the linguistic demands of the benefices they are ordained to serve which creates a chronic shortage of Welsh-speaking clergy.

The above difficulty is obvious to anyone familiar with the linguistic demography of Wales. There is, however, another less obvious difficulty, which is that, because of the high population density of areas with low proportions of Welsh speaking, and the low population density of areas with high proportions of Welsh speaking, many Welsh speakers reside in areas where the predominant language is English. This creates another problem for the Church. The obvious problem is ensuring a Welsh-speaking ministry to Welsh-speaking benefices. The less obvious problem is ensuring a ministry in the Welsh language to the large *number* of Welsh speakers in areas in which they form a small *proportion* of the population.

'Bilingualism' is an ambiguous term in the context of worship. It might be thought to imply 'dual provision': that is, the provision in each benefice of services wholly in Welsh and services wholly in English. It could equally be thought to imply a policy that every service should contain elements of each language. It is the latter policy that the Church in Wales has favoured. Underlying this decision are two considerations. The first is that there are degrees of ability to speak a language. Some non-native Welsh-speaking clergy have acquired the ability to conduct a service in Welsh but lack the ability to preach in that language. Such clergy can, at a pinch, be appointed to serve benefices with high levels of Welsh speaking in the absence of a native Welsh-speaking priest. They can also provide elements of worship in Welsh to cater for the needs of the large numbers of native Welsh speakers resident in predominantly English-speaking benefices. The second consideration is more subtle and more profound. A policy of 'dual provision' would in effect divide and separate the Anglican community in a benefice into different linguistic groups. This may be regarded as unacceptable on two grounds. First, it runs counter to the theological principle that believers are 'all one in Christ Jesus' and that Christianity transcends secular social divisions. Secondly, it runs counter to the inclusive nature of the Church as a 'church' in the technical sociological sense. More positively, the Church regards it to be part of its mission to heal the historic divisions not only between the Welsh and English but also between the Welsh-speaking Welsh and the monoglot English-speaking Welsh. Such divisions cannot be overcome merely by the inclusion of these different groups in the same institution, if they are not transcended within the local social group (the benefice).

The survey of benefices asked a number of detailed questions about the use of language in services. The data provided demonstrate that in practice only a small minority of benefices (15 per cent) opt for the 'dual-provision' solution, holding services in both languages, each service being wholly in Welsh or wholly in English. On the other hand, only 22 per cent had service patterns which were, in whole or part, bilingual. The majority of benefices, 63 per cent, held services all of which were solely in English. Only a tiny minority – 0.3 per cent – held services all of which were solely in Welsh.

It appears from these data that, while the Church has been relatively successful in avoiding the 'dual-provision' solution, it has been less successful in fostering bilingualism. The difficulties concerning the supply of Welsh-speaking clergy are shown by the fact that only 37 per cent of benefices have any Welsh-language provision at all, a figure very close to that for the proportion of incumbents who can preach in Welsh (34 per cent). This is higher than the proportion of Welsh speakers in the population (which affects the supply of Welsh-speaking clergy) and is slightly above the proportion of benefices which have populations of which more than 20 per cent speak Welsh. Of these benefices 84 per cent are rural benefices. However, 58 per cent of benefices have congregations of which more than 5 per cent speak Welsh. Half of these are in urban areas, and in such areas less than a quarter have any Welsh-language provision at all. This situation will not be improved by the fact that Welsh speaking among clergy is positively related to age, 40 per cent of those over sixty being able to preach in Welsh, as compared to only 30 per cent of those under sixty.

Membership
This is not the place to discuss the complexities of defining and measuring memberships of religious denominations, or even those peculiar to the Anglican Communion. The basic point that needs to be made, however, is that adherence to a denomination is a continuum. The data used in this study concentrate on practice rather than membership. It was intended that they should answer the following questions: how many people demonstrate allegiance to the Church through communicating at Easter, through attendance at weekly services, or by holding some office or responsibility within the benefice? The answers to these questions show the large variation between benefices in terms of the numbers of their adherents that has already been marked in our discussion of the ecclesiastical classification.

Benefices ranged in the number of their Easter communicants (ECs) from 14 to 1,000, the 10 per cent of benefices with the smallest number of ECs having fewer than 68, and the 10 per cent with the largest number of ECs having more than 338. The average number of ECs was 191, with 50 per cent of benefices having fewer than 156. On the other hand, 'congregational size', measured by averaging the communicants on two selected Sundays, ranged from single figures to around 500. The average figure for communicants was approximately 75, but with 50 per cent of benefices having 60 communicants or fewer. Again, strikingly, attendances ranged from below 22 (the lowest 10 per cent of benefices) to over 140 (the highest 10 per cent). Also exhibiting great variation was the number of lay workers, for this ranged from 1 to 90, the average being 18, with 50 per cent of benefices having fewer than 15 such laity.

Even if we ignore the highest and lowest figures, which are those of exceptional benefices, and concentrate on the figures which mark the boundaries of the lowest and highest 10 per cent, we find that benefices at the top of the distribution have attendance figures five or six times greater than those at the bottom. What are also of interest and importance are the average values and the extent of variation in three key ratios: the proportion formed by ECs of the general population, the proportion formed by the congregational size (average communicants) of ECs, and the proportion of the congregation formed by active lay participants.

In calculating the first of these ratios, total population figures have been used, since the figures for benefice populations of adults over the age of fourteen were not available. The proportion of the total benefice populations formed by Easter communicants ranged from below 1.5 per cent (the lowest 10 per cent of benefices) to above 14.7 per cent (the highest 10 per cent); in 50 per cent of benefices, the proportion was below 4.2 per cent. As we have seen, ECs are the most inclusive of the membership measures used in this study: they are an indication of the most minimal participation in Church life. Variation in the ratio of ECs to population is not primarily a reflection of local variation in the relative strength of the Church as opposed to that of other denominations. Since the Church in Wales is represented in every locality throughout the Province, it is primarily a reflection of local variation in the degree of secularity of the different civil populations to which the Church ministers. These figures show the extent to which the Church is *de facto* 'disestablished' among the populations in which it is set, and what is more important about them than their level is their range. An active membership of more than one in seven is, in a modern, differentiated society, impressive; a membership of less than 1.5 per cent is pretty exiguous.

The proportion of ECs (taken as 'all members') formed by average communicants (congregational size) ranged from below 19 per cent (the lowest 10 per cent of benefices) to above 60 per cent (the highest 10 per cent of benefices), 50 per cent of benefices having proportions below 40 per cent. This distribution is in marked contrast to that of the proportion of ECs to population. Both the average figures and the patterns of variation differ: whereas, in the case of the EC/population ratio, benefices cluster at the bottom of the range, in the case of the ratio of congregation size to ECs, benefices cluster at the top of the range. However, the main point to emerge is that in the contemporary Church there is a tendency for ECs to form a relatively small part of the population but for congregations to form an altogether larger proportion of ECs. The implication is that adherents defined in this way are very much a minority of the population, and approaching half of them attend only on the major festivals. On the other hand, the figures suggest that a minority of benefices can be identified where ECs form a significantly larger proportion of the population but weekly congregations form only a small part of those attending on major festivals.

The proportion of the weekly congregation formed by 'lay workers' (those having some office or responsibility within a benefice) ranged from below 18 per cent (the lowest 10 per cent of benefices) to above 55 per cent (the highest 10 per cent). Half of the benefices had proportions above 23 per cent. Hence this measure exhibits a smaller range of variation than the previous one, with bunching of benefices towards the bottom of the range. Clearly, since the number of offices and functions does not increase proportionately with congregational size, the proportion formed by lay workers will only be high in exceptionally small congregations.

Baptisms, funerals, confirmations

In the year before the survey, 15,136 persons were baptized in the responding benefices: that is, 25 baptisms per benefice. This compares with 15,100 funerals in the same period. This even balance might be regarded as a sign that the Church was replacing its membership lost by deaths. However, these figures must not be taken as 'membership' figures. Because of the Church's past status as an established Church, many of those being buried were not members in any effective sense. Equally, those being baptized as infants do not necessarily become effective members of the Church in later life, even so far as completing their Christian initiation through confirmation in their adolescent years. The number of confirmations during the same period numbered only 5,577 (ten per benefice), a little over one-third of the number of baptisms. Success in bringing all those baptized to confirmation would effectively halt the decline in membership noted in the previous chapter, always provided that those confirmed continued to demonstrate their adherence by communicating at the major festivals. Though the survey figures cannot demonstrate this, there can be little doubt, however, that further loss of effective membership occurs after confirmation, which is becoming for some a rite which marks the end of religious commitment rather than its beginning.

The extent of retention of membership between baptism and confirmation is indicated by the ratio of confirmations to baptisms. This measure cannot, however, be used to estimate the success of a benefice in bringing its baptized members to confirmation, for two reasons. In the first place, a success measure would need to calculate the ratio of confirmations to baptisms in the same age group (with a small allowance for mortality) – not, as in this survey, the ratio of confirmations to baptisms in the same year. Secondly, even if this were to be done, a low proportion in a given benefice might be the result of a net out-migration of families with young people, and a high proportion the result of net in-migration. Indeed, it is possible, as a result of the latter circumstance, for a benefice to have a number of confirmations which is greater than 100 per cent of the number of baptisms. Variation between benefices in the measure used here is, therefore, a result of change in levels of baptism and confirmation over time, and of population flows over time, as well as of the past efforts made by the benefice to bring baptized persons to confirmation. The result of these several factors has, however, been to create markedly different situations with regard to baptisms and confirmations in different benefices. The ratio of confirmations to baptisms – expressed as a percentage – ranges from below

1 per cent in the lowest 20 per cent of benefices to over 130 per cent in the top 10 per cent of benefices, half the benefices having proportions below 35 per cent. These proportions do not vary significantly with the *secular type*, but some relationship was found between them and the *ecclesiastical classification*. The less advantaged the benefice, the greater was the proportion having very low ratios, implying that some benefices suffered from a lack of resources in their efforts to bring baptized members to confirmation.

A need for information and effective organization

This chapter has been concerned primarily with the classification and typification of the benefices of the Church in Wales. Attention has centred on the attempt to generate categories and measures which make possible a description of a territorially organized religious institution. Such categories and measures were found necessary because the distributions of benefices by their attributes are such that summary statistics (such as averages) tend to conceal more than they reveal.

As far as we are aware, this task of classification has not been attempted before, either by sociologists of religion or by territorially organized Churches themselves. Once it is completed, however, it is then possible to use the descriptors which have been devised to generate data which could form part of what is today termed a 'management information system'. The creation of such a system is not regarded favourably by all those within the Church, since it implies that the Church is an 'organization' which has to be 'managed' (Beveridge 1971). This image is inconsistent with the way the Church is experienced by its members, whether clerical or lay. It is for them a moral community, a spiritual fellowship, a divine institution. It is seen as composed of unique persons and unique local communities, whose individuality is denied by categorization and classification. Its social order is held to be divinely instituted and not a means devised by humans to attain pragmatic ends. In sociological parlance, its social order is moral, not technical, and the Church is not, therefore, from the standpoint of its members or from that of sociology, an 'organization'.

We have argued elsewhere (Harris and Startup 1996b) for precisely this conclusion. A church, *qua* 'church', is not an 'organization'. However, it does not follow that a church does not *have* organization. Indeed, if it is to continue to exist it *must* have organization. This is so for two reasons. First, if the Church is a 'fellowship', then its members form a social group whereby those members are related to one another. If that fellowship is a 'household of faith', then the relationships between the members of that household need to be ordered and their activites co-ordinated. Secondly, as every member of the Church, from the secretary of a parochial church council (PCC) to the archbishop and the chairman of the Representative Body (RB), is acutely aware, the Church requires material resources to accomplish its mission and those resources have to be managed. If the Church is the 'Body of Christ', then through it the moral and the spritual are incarnate, embodied in the material. It is located in space and time, in history and society, and that location has to correspond to the locations of those to whom it is sent. If people and parishes are individuated (and this chapter has demonstrated just how far, in many respects, benefices do differ) and these different units form parts of a greater whole, if there are many gifts but the same Spirit, then what sociologists call 'the organic analogy' applies to the Church as a social group (as St Paul recognized) just as much as to 'society'. In consequence, those entrusted with the oversight of the whole – those, whether clerical or lay, who exercise some form of *episcope*, whatever its scope – have to make decisions, not necessarily about the normative order of the household of faith but about how that order is to be embodied in the here and now. To do this they need to understand the nature of the here and now, both secular and ecclesiastical.

It is one of the deficiencies of that mode of thought which goes by the name of 'modernity' and which originated in the Enlightenment, that it makes too absolute a divide between the moral and the technical. Judgements about the rightness of a course of action have to take into account not only its intrinsic properties but also its likely consequences. Judgements about the nature of those consequences require information about the context in which the action is to take place. To act in ignorance of the probable consequences of one's action is morally irresponsible. The right ordering of the life of a Church requires, therefore, that those who have to take decisions which affect it are appropriately informed. This chapter has described the means employed to provide information about the Church in Wales which was judged needful to inform its actions in the 1990s, a decade which the Lambeth Conference had proclaimed a 'decade of evangelism'. It will be the task of the next chapter to describe the larger units of the Church in Wales in the terms set out above. The same measures and categories can, however, also be employed, as is done in Chapter 4, to analyse the relations between the attributes of benefices so as to provide a deeper understanding of the situation of the Church.

LIBRARY, UNIVERSITY COLLEGE CHESTER

3

The Diversity of the Welsh Church:
the dioceses compared

Introduction

This chapter is concerned to provide a description of the Church in Wales in terms of the characteristics of the benefices that compose it. The relationships between these characteristics are explored through an examination and comparison of the different dioceses and archdeaconries into which the Church is divided for pastoral and administrative purposes. We consider patterns in benefice characteristics as these affect the territorial organization of the Church.

While many people resident in England underestimate the size of Wales, it is none the less a relatively small country. Given that this is so, the degree of variation within Wales – topographically, linguistically, economically – is remarkable, as any attempt to divide the Principality into sub-regions demonstrates. The variation between constituencies in both turnout and voting pattern in the 1997 referendum on the Welsh Assembly serves to emphasize this point.

Since the Industrial Revolution, if not before it, the historical division into north-west, north-east, south-west and south-east has become untenable. This has been largely due to developments in southern Wales. Whereas in north Wales the industrialization of the north-east tended to emphasize the ancient divide between east and west, the industrialization of the south made impossible any division into two, since as well as affecting the eastern part, which came to be centred on Cardiff, it also affected part of the west, which itself became divided into two when it developed an industrial area centred on Swansea.

At the same time the boundary to the east became unclear with the development of manufacturing centred on Newport, which blurred the traditional boundary between the ancient counties of Glamorgan and Monmouthshire. The ancient county of Monmouthshire (the 1974 county of Gwent) nevertheless remains very different both culturally and economically from the (1974) counties of Mid and South Glamorgan. To these problems have to be added those of mid-Wales, which may be defined as that area of Wales to the north of the Brecon Beacons and to the south of the Berwyn range which lies outside the catchment areas of Carmarthen and Aberystwyth and approximates to the (1974) county of Powys.

As described in Chapter 1, at its disestablishment in 1920 the Church in Wales comprised the four dioceses of Bangor, St Asaph, St Davids and Llandaff, but shortly afterwards the Church created two new dioceses, Swansea and Brecon, and Monmouth, thereby recognizing the distinctiveness of the western part of industrialized south Wales and of Monmouthshire, while following the principle that a diocese should contain a mix of rural and urban areas. This principle is, however, based on an underlying assumption about the relation between town and country: namely, that the country is the hinterland of a market town, or the travel-to-work area of an industrial one. Combining rural-agricultural and urban-industrial areas into one administrative unit may make sense, but if there is no organic relation between the different areas they do not constitute a base for any kind of communal life. The creation of Swansea and Brecon has been a successful solution to the problem of dealing administratively with the sparsely populated areas of the southern part of mid-Wales and providing pastoral oversight to their parish priests, but it cannot be said to have created a Christian community which straddles the Brecon Beacons. Moreover, the diocese's creation was only a partial solution to the 'mid-Wales' problem since it left untouched the southern parts of the dioceses of Bangor and St Asaph, which lie within mid-Wales. These areas do not form parts of the geographical areas centred on Bangor or the coastal towns of north-east Wales and have a quite different economic, cultural and linguistic composition. Moreover, they are a very long way from the diocesan centres in an area which lacks railways, motorways or even dual carriageways and is subject to extremes of weather. The remoteness of the southern parts of the two northern dioceses is eloquently grasped by the custom at one time prevalent in the diocese of Bangor of referring to its southernmost parts (not unkindly) as 'Outer Mongolia'.

It was with such considerations in mind that, in 1971, the then Archbishop of Wales, Glyn Simon, established a commission on the 'Structure and Boundaries of the Church in Wales'. This is not the place to go into the history of that commission, whose final report was not produced until 1978 and was not debated by the GB of the Church in Wales until 1980. It is sufficient to note here that the commission was faced with the choice between tinkering with diocesan boundaries and recommending radical change not only of boundaries but of the very structure of the political and geographical organization of the Church, something that Archbishop Simon clearly had in mind when he named the commission in the first place. (See the Archbishop's address to the Church's GB in September 1970 (Simon 1970).)

It is to the commission's credit, whatever view is taken of the wisdom of its proposals, that it did propose radical change, first by suggesting in an interim report the creation of a mid-Wales diocese (famously described by the then bishop of Swansea and Brecon as 'a sausage' and by another speaker from the same diocese as 'populated mainly by sheep') and a diocese corresponding to the (then) new county of West Glamorgan with its cathedral in Swansea. The similarity of these proposals to elements of the then recent but unpopular pattern of local government reorganization, as well as the opposition of those to be affected by the proposed changes, proved their undoing. The final proposals were even more radical. They involved the creation of a large north Wales diocese and a large south-east diocese. These new dioceses were to be presided over by a college of bishops, the latter notion deriving from a report of the Church of England's Advisory Council for the Church's Ministry (1971), each bishop having his own 'bishopric' (area of pastoral jurisdiction), one of the college being the administrative head of the whole. The commission's proposals also involved the extension of the diocese of Swansea and Brecon to include Neath and Port Talbot, and its subdivision into two bishoprics, Swansea and Brecon, the latter becoming the archiepiscopal see. These proposals were decisively rejected by the GB in July 1980.

This long-drawn-out episode illustrates the difficulty for

Church organization posed by the diversity of Wales, not only in spite of its relatively small geographical compass and population but also because of it. In an administrative and pastoral system with only six main parts (dioceses), any major change in the relation between any two of the parts is likely to have consequences for the whole.

In the Church in Wales, as in all episcopally ordered Churches, the diocese is the basic unit of organization and of clergy deployment. Each has, therefore, to comprise enough benefices for there to be significant variation between them, so that clergy may be deployed in such a way that the varying attributes of individual clergy match those required by the demands of different benefices. This requires that a diocese be relatively large. It is also an area of the *episcope*, literally 'oversight', of the bishop. As we have seen, the bishop is responsible for the ministry exercised by his vicars in the parishes of the diocese and for their pastoral care. This requires that the diocese be not too large in terms of the number of clergy for the chief shepherd to know the ordained members of his flock and call them by name, and not too extensive in area for him to maintain contact with them and their parishes.

A diocese is also a unit of administration, as the origin of the term implies. It is responsible for funding the payment of its clergy and supervising the management of its property. This requires that it have its own central administration, which in turn has to be funded. It is therefore a unit for the raising of revenue, which is done by a levy on benefices called the 'diocesan quota'. The maintenance of the presence of the Church in small, poor benefices requires that there be some mechanism whereby subvention from richer to poorer benefices is possible. The diocese is the unit within which such subventions occur, via the mechanism of the 'quota', whose incidence varies according to the size of congregation. For these purposes also, dioceses have to be reasonably large and contain benefices which vary significantly in terms of the size of their congregations and incomes. It is apparent, therefore, that dioceses as well as benefices have to be 'viable', and for dioceses this means that they have to be viable in terms of the number and variability (on the dimensions of congregational size and income) of the benefices that they comprise.

The fact that the bulk of the cost of the ministry is paid out of central funds (the dioceses only being required to fund the balance), while it renders the problem of supporting the small, poor benefices less acute, does not obviate it. In every diocese there are some benefices which could not continue to function if the financial requirements of the diocese were met by dividing the sum required equally among its benefices. Moreover, the mechanism for subsidizing the ministry in each diocese from central funds involves merely the payment of a proportion of the cost of the employment of each ordained minister, ignoring diocesan differences in ability to pay the residue. In other words, the subvention from rich to poor does not take place between, as opposed to within, dioceses – an arrangement which assumes that the dioceses contain within them similar distributions of benefices in terms of economic advantage. However, the diversity of the different areas of Wales to which the dioceses correspond results in dioceses having different distributions of their benefices on many attributes. At the same time the large extent of each of the six dioceses – and the fact that they were constructed so as to combine both urban and rural, and more and less affluent, areas – disguises the differences, both ecclesiastical and secular, between different parts of the Province as a whole.

The purpose of this chapter is not, however, to demonstrate the diversity of benefices, which is dealt with in detail in Chapters 2 and 4; it is, rather, to describe the diversity of the six dioceses of the Church (Bangor, St Asaph, St Davids, Swansea and Brecon, Llandaff and Monmouth) and the fourteen archdeaconries that constitute subdivisions of them, using the attributes of the benefices that compose them. (Since some archdeaconries have the same names as dioceses the suffix 'a/d' (archdeaconry) is occasionally used below to avoid ambiguity.)

Secular characteristics of dioceses

As far as secular characteristics are concerned, it is possible to divide the Province into two main areas. Llandaff and Monmouth contain proportionately more benefices with populations of above 4,500, and densities of over three persons per hectare, while St Asaph, Bangor and St Davids have relatively more benefices with populations of under 4,500 and densities of below three persons per hectare. Swansea and Brecon approximates to the provincial average.

Swansea and Brecon is, however, made up of two very different areas. The archdeaconry of Brecon has more benefices with very small populations than the most rural dioceses: its median benefice population is below that of any other archdeaconry, lower even than those of the archdeaconries of Cardigan and Montgomery. No less than two-fifths of the benefices in Brecon archdeaconry have populations of under 850. On the other hand, the proportion of its benefices with very low *densities* is below those of three other archdeaconries: Montgomery, Merioneth, and Cardigan. By contrast, Gower, the other archdeaconry in the diocese of Swansea and Brecon, which approximates the new (1995) City and County of Swansea, has a high proportion of benefices with populations exceeding 6,000, as do the archdeaconry of Newport and both of Llandaff's archdeaconries. Gower is also among the three archdeaconries having the highest population densities. It is clear that, in categorizing the ecclesiastical areas of the Province, Swansea and Brecon's two archdeaconries must be treated separately, Gower belonging with the more urban dioceses and Brecon with the more rural ones.

A similar problem attaches to the diocese of Monmouth. Monmouth archdeaconry has a very low benefice population size, only slightly higher than Brecon, but is not characterized by exceptionally low density. By contrast, Newport has the highest proportion of benefices with very high sizes and densities and is, on these criteria, the most 'urbanized' archdeaconry in the Province, belonging with Llandaff diocese and Gower archdeaconry.

Whereas the difference between the dioceses in terms of the size and density distributions of their benefice populations is not great, when archdeaconries are examined four stand out as having, relatively speaking, high proportions of benefices with very low size and density: in the diocese of Bangor, Merioneth; in St Asaph, Montgomery; in Swansea and Brecon, Brecon; and in St Davids, Cardigan. All except the last belong to what has been defined above as 'mid-Wales'.

This complex picture is simplified by the 'secular type' classification (see pp. 30–2), which combines population size and density measures. The four most urban archdeaconries (large population, high density), namely Newport, Margam, Gower, and Llandaff, are those which have the largest proportion of benefices in the three highest (most urban) categories of the secular type classification. None of the other archdeaconries has even one-fifth of its benefices in these categories. The five most rural archdeaconries (small population, low density), namely Brecon, Montgomery, Cardigan, Merioneth, and St Davids, are those which have the highest proportions of benefices in the three lowest (most rural) categories. On the other hand, St Asaph archdeaconry has a distribution of benefices which is average for the Province, while the remaining four archdeaconries – Wrexham, Bangor a/d, Carmarthen, and Monmouth – are over-represented in the middle secular-type categories.

The not unexpected pattern which emerges is that archdeaconries within mid-Wales and on the south-west coast are the most rural, and those along the eastern south coast most urban. What is particularly significant is that the organization of the Church into dioceses is such that those of Llandaff and Monmouth have no archdeaconry in the most rural category, while three dioceses possess no archdeaconry in the most urban category. The dioceses of St Asaph, Bangor, and St Davids could be described, therefore, as 'non-urban' rather than rural because their rural archdeaconries are balanced by middling archdeaconries (but not by urban ones), and the diocese of Monmouth may be termed 'non-rural' because its urban archdeaconry is not balanced by a rural one. Only the diocese of Llandaff is genuinely urban, with both archdeaconries in the urban category. Again, Swansea and Brecon is the only diocese to combine two archdeaconries at the extremes of the urban–rural continuum. The failure to do this elsewhere is the result of the absence of any sufficiently large urban areas outside industrial south Wales to balance other predominantly rural areas. The inability to achieve the desired urban–rural balance has consequences for the distribution of resources between dioceses, as we shall see.

Secular characteristics and grouping

One of the responses of the Church to the problems posed by the existence of many parishes with small populations and large areas (low size-density) has been the grouping of parishes into benefices. Table 3.1 shows the proportion of group benefices: that is, the *level* of grouping in each diocese. The urban diocese of Llandaff has the lowest figure, while the three dioceses characterized above as 'non-urban' have the highest level of grouping. The same type of pattern is evident in respect of archdeaconries. In particular, the four archdeaconries whose benefices are substantially over-represented among those with the lowest density in the whole province (Brecon, Cardigan, Merioneth and Montgomery) have the highest proportion of grouped benefices, and the grouping order corresponds to the density order. Both population size and density would appear to be important factors determining the level of grouping. In the Province as a whole, we find that only 17 per cent of benefices with low (i.e. below median) densities are single benefices, compared with 72 per cent of benefices with high densities. The figures as regards population size are very similar. Only 24 per cent of benefices with low (i.e. below median) population sizes are single benefices, compared with 65 per cent of those with high population sizes.

Table 3.1   Group benefices in each diocese

Diocese	Group benefices* as % of all benefices	Group benefices* comprising non-viable parishes as % of all benefices
St Asaph	52.1	20.2
Bangor	78.6	50.0
St Davids	73.5	42.7
Llandaff	27.3	4.1
Monmouth	39.0	15.8
Swansea & Brecon	53.9	37.2
PROVINCE	52.2	26.3

*other than rectorial benefices.

Five archdeaconries were markedly below average in their proportion of grouped benefices: Newport, Margam, Gower, Llandaff archdeaconry, and Wrexham. When we put these archdeaconries in rank order according to their proportion of group benefices, we find that the order does not reflect their secular-type rank. Margam and Wrexham had fewer, and

Llandaff more, group benefices than would be expected on the basis of their size and density. This conclusion will not surprise those familiar with urban sociology, for it is well established that while the constraints of low size and density tend to make rural places in many respects similar to one another, the removal of those constraints at the other end of the rural–urban continuum makes possible choice, and hence variation, between places having the same high densities and large population sizes. In the present instance, departures of the more urban archdeaconries from their expected levels of grouping are likely to reflect differences between them in their past and present diocesan policies in the creation of group benefices.

Type of grouping
Two types of group benefices were distinguished: viable and non-viable. Secular factors relate not merely to grouping as such but also to the type of group formed. Table 3.1 shows that the proportion of all benefices in each diocese formed by group benefices comprising non-viable parishes was highest in the dioceses of Bangor and St Davids, followed by Swansea and Brecon, and lowest in the diocese of Llandaff, followed by Monmouth and St Asaph. On the other hand, the archdeaconries with the highest proportions of all benefices which were groups of non-viable parishes were, in ascending order, St Davids a/d (43 per cent), Merioneth (48 per cent), Bangor a/d (52 per cent), Cardigan (57 per cent), and Brecon (67 per cent). This last figure makes clear that the contribution from Brecon accounts for the unexpectedly large Swansea and Brecon diocese figure.

Larger size and higher density make choice possible. Non-viable parishes *have* to be grouped; viable parishes may be grouped through choice rather than necessity. To examine this aspect of grouping we need to explore the proportion not of all benefices but of *group* benefices which comprise viable and non-viable parishes. The diocese most prone to group viable parishes is Llandaff, 85 per cent of whose group benefices were classified as composed of viable parishes, followed by St Asaph (61 per cent), and Monmouth (58 per cent). The other three dioceses seem to have grouped chiefly on the grounds of non-viability. In St Davids 58 per cent of group benefices are composed of non-viable parishes, in Bangor 64 per cent, and in Swansea and

Brecon 69 per cent. An examination of the figures for archdea-conries shows that, while two of the four archdeaconries with the highest proportion of benefices with lowest sizes and densities predominantly group non-viable parishes (Cardigan and Bangor archdeaconry), the other two archdeaconries are either near (Merioneth) or substantially below (St Davids a/d) the provincial average.

Taking the Province as a whole, however, as Table 3.2 shows, we find a fairly strong correlation between both the grouping measures and 'secular type', the classification of settlements used in this study. The evident tendency is for the proportion of benefices which are groups to rise with rurality, while the proportion of those groups comprising viable parishes declines. However, it is not simply this overall pattern that is our central concern. This chapter is scrutinizing the Church as a territorial organization. We are concerned to examine the variation between dioceses and archdeaconries in terms of their secular characteristics, and the consequences of those characteristics for Church organization. In so doing we demonstrate the distinctiveness of different dioceses and archdeaconries.

Table 3.2   **The grouping of benefices and** *secular type*

	Grouping	
Secular type	*Extent* *% of all benefices* *which are groups*	*Type* *% of group benefices* *comprising viable parishes*
city	16	81
large town	11	100
urban aggregation	40	100
large rural nucleated	53	70
small rural nucleated	65	58
large rural dispersed	95	43
small rural dispersed	85	18

The figures for archdeaconries concerning type of grouping imply that the heterogeneity with which the Church has to cope exists not only between dioceses and between archdeaconries but even within archdeaconries themselves. For example, it would appear that grouping occurs within archdeaconries for both policy and rural necessity reasons, even where the archdeaconry is characterized by a large proportion of very rural benefices. This does not upset their position in the rank order in terms of the level of grouping, but it does upset their position in the order according to their type. There is, though, another factor which increases the propensity to group viable parishes in low-density areas, and that is the need to provide ministry in Welsh. High rates of Welsh speaking are associated with low population size and density areas, and in such areas parishes may be grouped to provide a ministry in Welsh even where the parishes concerned are viable. It is for this reason, rather than for reasons of policy, that some rural archdeaconries have higher than expected proportions of groupings which comprise viable parishes.

Ecclesiastical characteristics

We are now ready to describe the Province in terms of our 'ecclesiastical classification' which ranks benefices from 'large, rich' to 'small, poor', distinguishing also in the former case benefices according to numbers of stipendiary clergy, and in the latter benefices comprising varying numbers of parishes. Table 3.3 characterizes both dioceses and archdeaconries in terms of the categories of the classification in which their benefices are over-represented. The categories of the classification were given numbers to allow the calculation of a score for each area, indicating the degree of its advantage. The numbers ranged from six for a large, rich benefice with two or more clergy to one for a small, poor benefice with three or more parishes (for the six categories, see Table 2.2).

Llandaff diocese is clearly the most advantaged in terms of the resources of its benefices. It is substantially over-represented in the top two categories of advantage and under-represented in all other categories, most substantially in the lowest category of advantage. By the same criterion, the most disadvantaged diocese is St Davids, which is substantially over-represented in the least advantaged category and under-represented in the four most advantaged categories. In terms of the pattern of distribution of benefices over the categories of the ecclesiastical classification, and in terms of the overall advantage score, Swansea and Brecon

Table 3.3   The over-representation of dioceses and
archdeaconries among categories of the *ecclesiastical
classification* (implying relative resource advantage/
disadvantage)

Area	Advantage		Category of benefices over-represented	Degree of over-representation (actual % less expected %)
	score	rank		
Llandaff	4.2	1	large, rich	19
Monmouth	3.7	2	rich	5
Swansea & Brecon	3.6	3	large	4
St Asaph	3.4	4	small, poor	9
Bangor	3.3	5	large, poor	9
St Davids	3.2	6	small, poor	14
PROVINCE	3.6	–	–	–
Archdeaconries in rank order of advantage				
Llandaff		1	large, rich	30
Gower		2	large, rich	22
Margam		3	large, rich	8
			small, rich	5
Newport		4	large, rich; 2 or more clergy	13
			large, poor	8
St Asaph		5	Prov. dist., but large, poor	10
Bangor		6	Prov. dist., but large, poor	5
			small, poor; 3 or more parishes	6
Carmarthen		7	Prov. dist., but large rich; 1 clergy	5
			small, poor; 3 or more parishes	8
Monmouth		8	large, rich; 1 clergy	13
			small, rich	16
			small, poor; 3 or more parishes	10
Merioneth		9	large, poor	13
St Davids		10	small, poor; 3 or more parishes	17
Wrexham		11	small, poor; 1 or 2 parishes	16
Brecon		12	small, poor	21
			of which 3 or more parishes	18
Montgomery		13	small, poor	26
Cardigan		14	small, poor	30

and Monmouth approximate the provincial pattern, Monmouth
having a slight edge, with rather more large, rich parishes and
slightly fewer small, poor ones. The remaining two dioceses have
an advantage score significantly below the provincial average. St
Asaph is under-represented in the large rich categories and over-
represented among the small, poor categories. Bangor is likewise
under-represented among the large, rich categories but, by

contrast to St Asaph, is over-represented in the large, poor category rather than in the small, poor category.

The tendency for dioceses to approximate the provincial average results from there being included within them contrasting areas which balance one another in terms of advantage, as the figures for archdeaconries illustrate. The two exceptions are St Davids and Llandaff. In Llandaff's case small benefices tend to be 'rich' and poor benefices 'large' so that few benefices are disadvantaged in terms of both size and income. At the same time Llandaff has virtually no (0.8 per cent) low-density areas to promote multi-parish groupings. By contrast, in St Davids a quarter of all benefices are in the least advantaged category ('small, poor', three or more parishes). Again, St Davids has two highly disadvantaged archdeaconries, Cardigan (rank 14) and St Davids a/d (rank 10), which are not balanced by any high-ranking archdeaconries, its Carmarthen archdeaconry being ranked only 7. Both Llandaff's archdeaconries, by contrast, are highly advantaged, being in the top three places in the rank order.

Having painted a picture of the diversity of the Province using the relatively broad brush of the secular type (population size-density) and ecclesiastical classification (degree of advantage), it is now possible to consider the attributes of benefices in slightly more detail.

Benefice incomes and expenditure patterns

Inequality between dioceses is reflected in differences in their distributions of benefice incomes. This is well illustrated by the proportion of benefices having incomes which fall in the range occupied by the extremes of the income distribution, as shown in Table 3.4. The differences are startling: almost one-third of the incomes in the diocese of Bangor fall into the range occupied by the 20 per cent of benefices with the lowest incomes in the Province (£1,500–£9,000), compared with under one-eighth of the incomes of benefices in Llandaff. If we consider not the 'poor' but the 'rich' and focus on proportions of incomes in the top 20 per cent of the Province's income range (£28,000–£100,000), the figures are almost exactly reversed.

When we turn to the way in which benefices in the different dioceses spend their incomes, we find that no head of expenditure

Table 3.4   Variations between dioceses in benefice income

	% of benefices in lowest 20% of provincial income distribution	% of benefices in highest 20% of provincial income distribution
St Asaph	23.7	16.2
Bangor	32.1	12.5
St Davids	24.1	13.8
Llandaff	11.7	34.5
Monmouth	13.6	33.4
Swansea & Brecon	19.5	14.3
PROVINCE	20.0	20.0

rivals the diocesan quota, the amount paid by a benefice to its diocese chiefly in support of clergy stipends. In only 8 per cent of all benefices in the province does the quota amount to less than 20 per cent of expenditure; in 46 per cent of benefices it amounts to more than one-third, and in 23 per cent to more than a half. Its only rival is expenditure on buildings, on which 33 per cent spend more than one-third, and 8 per cent more than half.

When we compare dioceses with respect to the proportion spent on the quota, we find that St Davids has the highest proportion of benefices where the quota accounts for over half the expenditure (42 per cent), followed by Bangor (27 per cent) and by Monmouth and Swansea and Brecon (both 21 per cent). In Llandaff and in St Asaph, by contrast, in only 12 and 13 per cent of benefices respectively does the quota account for more than half the expenditure. As might be expected, this rank order is, with one major exception, broadly similar to the rank order of advantage shown above in Table 3.3. In other words, the demands of the quota bear most heavily in the least advantaged dioceses. The exception is St Asaph, whose unexpected position does not seem to derive from its spending relatively more on any other particular item. It spends slightly more on all items other than the quota.

After providing for its clergy, the greatest financial burden on benefices is the maintenance of their buildings. The average benefice has 2.68 churches open for worship, and 1.39 other buildings. These figures vary substantially between dioceses, as

Table 3.5 shows. The two most disadvantaged dioceses (Bangor and St Davids) also have to maintain the largest number of churches. The two most advantaged dioceses (Llandaff and Monmouth) have the fewest churches to maintain, while St Asaph and Swansea and Brecon approximate to the provincial average. With regard to other buildings, Monmouth has most and is substantially above average, while St Asaph and Swansea and Brecon have fewest, the remaining three dioceses approximating to the provincial mean. It is debatable whether 'other buildings' should be regarded as a burden or a resource in financial terms, since they are not as expensive to maintain as churches and, unlike churches, are a source of income. In any case, dioceses show much less variation in number of buildings than in number of churches.

Table 3.5   Mean number of open churches and other buildings per benefice, by diocese

	Churches	Other
St Asaph	2.59	1.25
Bangor	3.73	1.43
St Davids	3.03	1.42
Llandaff	2.16	1.47
Monmouth	1.91	1.63
Swansea & Brecon	2.47	1.26
PROVINCE	2.68	1.39

Clergy and people

Having examined material resources and their patterns of use, we now turn to an examination of human resources. The prime resource is, of course, a diocese's clergy. Table 3.6 shows for each diocese the mean size of civil population, Easter communicants and congregational size, divided by the number of full-time, stipendiary, parochial clergy; the final column displays congregational size expressed as a proportion of Easter communicants. These data give some indication of the variation in 'clergy load' between the dioceses.

From the standpoint of the Anglican Church, the inhabitants

Table 3.6   Clergy load: civil population, Easter communicants (ECs) and congregation per cleric*

Diocese	Number per cleric of:			Weekly communicants as proportion of ECs (per cent)
	population	ECs	weekly communicants	
St Asaph	4330	184	61	33
Bangor	3540	179	59	35
St Davids	2802	169	58	34
Llandaff	6915	160	73	45
Monmouth	6032	120	55	46
Swansea & Brecon	3596	135	58	44
PROVINCE	4763	157	62	40

*i.e. full-time, stipendiary, parochial clergy

of a given area may be thought of as falling into the following religious categories: no religion; non-Christian affiliation; nominally Christian, no denominational affiliation; non-Anglican Christian affiliation; Anglican affiliation. This last category can then be subdivided into three main categories: on the one hand there are those whose affiliation is nominal (i.e. there is no attendance, except for rites of passage); on the other, there are those who are active – confirmed members of the Church who attend frequently; in between are those who are confirmed and attend only at the major festivals, the most important of which is Easter.

This standpoint points up the significance of the data in Table 3.6. The first column (population per cleric) gives the number of people who would be under the care of each cleric were there to be no religions other than the Christian religion, and no Christian religious denominations other than the Anglican. The ratio is a measure of the size of the responsibility of each cleric of an established national Church. The Church in Wales is disestablished and there are other denominations and religions. These figures are included here, however, because the hitherto established Anglican Church in Wales still considers itself responsible for the spiritual welfare of all the inhabitants of the Principality. In a perfect world, therefore, its parochial clergy should know enough about all the inhabitants of the area that they serve to enable them to ascertain whether or not each inhabitant belongs to another religion or denomination. The figures in the first column, therefore, estimate the average extent of each cleric's responsibilities for pastoral oversight.

The second column indicates the average size of the pastoral responsibility of each cleric for all communicant Anglicans in the area that is served; while the third indicates the average extent of each cleric's pastoral responsibilities in respect of the gathered congregation of active members. The final column of the table effectively expresses the average size of the regular congregation as a proportion of the average number of all communicating Anglicans.

In respect of population, the weight is heaviest in the two most urban dioceses (Monmouth and Llandaff) with loads substantially above the provincial average, least heavy in the two most rural dioceses (St Davids and Bangor), St Asaph occupying an intermediate position, with a load close to the provincial average. On this measure, however, Swansea and Brecon belongs with the relatively rural dioceses, having a load similar to that of Bangor, though not as light as that of St Davids.

As regards congregational load (weekly communicants) the third column of Table 3.6 shows that this is heaviest for clergy in Llandaff. There is little variation in this load between the remaining, less heavily loaded, dioceses. In respect of Easter communicants (all communicating Anglicans), the load is heaviest in the three relatively rural dioceses (St Asaph, Bangor, and St Davids) but also in Llandaff, and significantly lighter in Monmouth and in Swansea and Brecon.

When we consider the variation in loads of different types between the most heavily and least heavily loaded dioceses, we find that variation in congregational load is relatively small, the most heavily loaded diocese having a value which is only 131 per cent of the least heavily loaded. Variation in Easter communicant load is more considerable (154 per cent) but variation in population load is altogether greater, the most heavily loaded diocese (Llandaff) having a value which is no less than 247 per cent of the least heavily loaded (St Davids).

These figures highlight the central problem in the organization of the Province into dioceses and in provincial policy concerning the way these are resourced from central funds. The data in the present work were generated in order for the Church to prepare for the 1990s 'decade of evangelism'. In summary terms, the Church wished to shift its emphasis from maintenance to mission. The size of the evangelistic task, as measured by clergy load, varies between dioceses in both extent and character. The final column of Table 3.6 shows that in the more rural dioceses, which are relatively advantaged in terms of population load on clergy, the load imposed by the care of communicant Anglicans tends to be heavy. Conversely, in the more urban dioceses, where the load imposed by population is relatively heavy, that imposed by the care of communicant Anglicans is relatively light.

So far we have considered various measures of load on clergy. We have not considered qualitative differences between the dioceses in the task they face. Some light can be thrown on this issue by reference to the key membership ratios (introduced in Chapter 2) for the benefices of the different dioceses. The median proportion of the population who are communicant Anglicans is approximately 5 per cent in the Province as a whole. The proportions in the three relatively rural dioceses are higher, those in the two more urban dioceses lower. Swansea and Brecon straddles this divide, Brecon archdeaconry being over-represented among benefices with higher proportions, and Gower among those with lower proportions. In other words, the extent to which the population is at least nominally Anglican is greater in the countryside than in the towns.

When we consider the proportion of Easter communicants formed by average communicants (i.e. the regular congregation) we find that the more rural dioceses include relatively more benefices where this ratio is low (under 40 per cent; cf. the fourth column of Table 3.6). Conversely, the more urban dioceses include relatively more benefices where the regular congregation forms a higher proportion of Easter communicants (over 40 per cent). In Swansea and Brecon there are more benefices with proportions above 40 per cent and below 50 per cent, but none in the higher ranges. While urban Gower archdeaconry has a pattern similar in this respect to that of Llandaff and of Monmouth, it is not the case that rural Brecon has a pattern similar to that of the three more rural dioceses, since rather more of its benefices have ratios in the middle of the range.

The two ratios last considered together enable us to identify the distinctive character of the tasks facing benefices in different dioceses. In the rural areas where Anglicans form a larger proportion of the population, and congregations a smaller proportion of communicating Anglicans, the chief priority would seem to be transforming occasional into regular attenders. In the urban areas, where Anglicans form a smaller proportion of the population, and congregations a larger proportion of communicating Anglicans, the chief priority would seem to be the evangelization of the un-churched rather than of the churched. But are those outside the category of communicating Anglicans entirely 'un-churched'? If in rural areas the 'outreach' of the congregation is more often facilitated by the existence of a penumbra of occasional communicants than in urban areas, the outreach of urban congregations is extended by the contacts made through the use by the general population of what are called the 'occasional offices': baptisms, marriages and funerals, known colloquially as hatching, matching and dispatching, and academically as *rites de passage*. The total number of persons involved in such occasions during the year before the survey was 48,553 – a figure, as it happens, roughly the same size as that for regular Anglican attenders. While many of these services were conducted for those already Church members, it is likely that the bulk were not, and they constitute therefore a major evangelistic opportunity. Of greatest significance here is, obviously, baptisms.

In an ecclesiastically perfect world, numbers of baptisms and of subsequent confirmations should be of similar magnitude, since they are two stages in the process of Christian initiation. The third of our key ratio measures is the proportion formed by confirmations of baptisms in a given year (expressed as a percentage); this may be taken as a rough indicator of the extent of retention of membership between the two stages. In the Province as a whole confirmations formed 36.8 per cent of baptisms. This suggests that the Church is losing, very roughly, something in the order of 10,000 members a year through baptized persons not ratifying their baptisms through confirmation. The data also show significant differences between dioceses. The two most rural dioceses included relatively more benefices with above median ratios of confirmations to baptisms, while Monmouth contained proportionately more benefices with below median ratios, the remaining dioceses approximating to the provincial average. These figures suggest that if a key task facing the rural areas is to activate their occasional communicants, then a task of central importance facing the more urban areas is to capitalize on the contacts made through the occasional offices, especially baptism.

Conclusion

This chapter has demonstrated that resources vary in their distribution between dioceses. To facilitate the shift to 'mission', resources need to be distributed between dioceses in proportion to the evangelistic rather than the pastoral task. As far as clerical staffing is concerned, if evangelism is urgent because of the decline in the number of Easter communicants, then the size of the task of evangelism must be measured by the population/clergy load. This implies a transfer of resources from more rural dioceses with low loads, such as Bangor and St Davids, to the more urban dioceses of Llandaff and Monmouth. Conversely, if the immediate challenge is to bring into active membership all those who are communicating members of the Church (all Easter communicants), then the size of the task is best measured by the Easter communicant/clergy load. This implies shifting resources from dioceses such as Monmouth and Swansea and Brecon, where the EC load tends to be low, to the more rural dioceses of Bangor and St Asaph. Were the major policy imperative to be the pastoral care of regular congregations, then very little redistribution of clergy would be required, except a minor one in favour of Llandaff. The lesson to be learned from Table 3.6 is, therefore, that as far as the distribution of clergy is concerned, the present deployment reflects the imperative of maintenance rather than of various forms of mission.

It is not being suggested that those in positions of authority in the Church, both clerical and lay, are unaware of this fact. The continued distribution of resources that reflects the priority of maintenance over mission is the result of the combination of two other types of consideration. The first is that there are no means for effecting a provincial policy concerning the distribution of resources. The basic unit of Church organization is the diocese, and the creation of a disestablished Church in Wales separate from the Church of England did not 'unite' the Welsh dioceses but 'grouped' them. The dioceses are inferior to the central bodies of the Church only in respect of external affairs, doctrine, liturgy, legal regulation, and the holding of property. While the GB of the Church regulates the activities of dioceses and their components, it does not and cannot determine the direction of those activities. The dioceses are primarily dependent not upon the GB but upon the Representative Body of the Church in Wales, the legal organ that holds the Church's property, in so far as that body funds the major part of the costs of clergy benefits. However, the Representative Body is concerned only with the administration of the Church's property and does not and cannot use its control of central funds to impose policy upon dioceses.

The second consideration is that the task of maintaining the presence of the Church in rural areas is itself becoming extremely difficult, even with the present level of resources available to the more rural dioceses, as our discussion of grouping demonstrates. Any transfer of resources from more rural to more urban dioceses would jeopardize maintaining an Anglican presence throughout the more rural dioceses.

In sum, there is no constitutional mechanism for implementing a provincial policy of resource allocation, but if there were, and if it were designed to prioritize mission over maintenance, it would need to be informed by the kinds of analysis presented in this study. Such a policy would not be required were the magnitude of the tasks faced by all dioceses identical and the resources available to them equal. This chapter has, however, demonstrated the diversity of dioceses in terms of both task and resources. This problem is not peculiar to the Church in Wales, nor is it a distinctively Welsh, or even a distinctively ecclesiastical, problem. It is the problem of the relation between central and local political bodies wherever it is the case that the tasks faced by local areas are highly various (which provides a pragmatic argument for local autonomy) and the resources available to tackle those tasks vary markedly between localities (which provides a pragmatic argument for greater funding of local areas via a central body to make cross-subsidy possible).

This argument is, however, one which is narrowly conceived, since it refers to only two types of resource, money and clergy, and ignores other types of human resource, i.e. the laity. The solution to what are essentially organizational problems should not be sought, because it cannot be found, solely within the formal organizational structure of the Church; it should be sought within the content of that structure. That content is the concern of the second part of this book. Before that task is attempted, however, it is necessary to return the focus of our exploration of the contemporary Church to the basic unit of its social body, the benefice, which is the concern of the next chapter.

4

The benefices of the Church

It is a truism that we live today in a secular society, and sociologists have long debated what has come to be known as the 'secularization thesis'. This thesis is a corollary of the view that contemporary societies are, or are becoming, caught up in the process of 'modernization'. The modernist perspective, which involves an understanding of history and the process of social change as linear and directional has been increasingly challenged in recent years by those who have come to be called 'postmodernists'. As far as religion is concerned, the modernist view involves the assumption that modernization involves the replacement of religious by scientific modes of thought, and the decline of religious belief and practice. This is the core of what is meant by the 'secularization thesis', which finds itself under attack by the postmodernist denial of the directionality of social change.

As far as society is concerned, the movement towards modernity was not held to consist merely of cultural change. On the contrary, in sociological terms the key feature of the modernization process has always been held to involve increasing structural differentiation: the development of distinct and specialized social institutions, each having distinct functions (Hamilton 1995, ch. 15). For example, universities and schools were originally religious institutions; in the last 150 years they have become separated from religious institutions and now subserve cultural and scientific rather than religious functions. At different points in history, religious institutions became separated from political institutions, and both from economic institutions, and all three from the institutions of kinship. This process of differentiation can be expressed in the language of 'loss': for example, it may be claimed that the family has 'lost' its productive, religious and political functions. It is equally the case, however, that the State has 'lost' its basis in kinship, its religious legitimation and many of its former economic functions. If all the chief social institutions have separated out, then each one, and not just religion, may be said to have 'lost' what are now the functions of the others.

This process of separation creates a social situation whereby each institution can be defined in opposition to the others. For example, the idea that the Church should not 'interfere' in politics – very much a modern idea, which our ancestors would have found very puzzling – involves the assumption that if anything is political it is not religious, and vice versa. Moreover, it is easy to slip into thinking of the types of institutional groups that make up society as being exclusive. However, though the terms 'Welsh' and 'Scots' denote exclusive groups – you can belong to one or the other but not both – it is not the case that if you are a politician you cannot be a church member or a family member or occupy a position in the economic structure. On the contrary, every member of society can be said to occupy a position in each of these social spheres.

Whether or not our society is undergoing an inevitable process of secularization, it certainly has undergone a process of institutional differentiation, and this makes it possible to attribute a distinctly social meaning to the Christian distinction between 'church' and 'world'. In Christian discourse 'world' has always had two distinct meanings: negative and positive. On the one hand there was the 'world' which (in the Anglican Communion) Christian initiates used to renounce at their baptism along with the 'flesh' and the Devil; on the other was the 'world' as the totality of God's creation, which Genesis told them to regard as 'good', and for which, St John told them, Christ died.

With the process of institutional differentiation, another meaning became available. 'World' came to refer to that part of society which was not the Church, and this particular identification meant that the negative Christian definition of the 'world' tended to outweigh the positive: if the world was not the Church, which was by definition good, then the world must be bad. Once these shifts in meaning have occurred it becomes possible to ignore what is bad within the Church, to regard the Church as somewhere to withdraw to and the world as a place to withdraw from, rather than as a place to which Christians are sent. The result is the development of a tendency to ignore the fact that the

Church is part of the world – God's creation – and, simultaneously, part of the society in which it exists. The Church is not
merely set over against the rest of society that is not the Church.
What is being claimed here is that changes in the structure of
society have had consequences for the way in which the language
of Christian belief works. These changes have affected all denominations, particularly in the nineteenth century, and have, in turn,
evoked a reaction in the twentieth.

These issues will arise again when we come to discuss the attitudes of the laity in the Church in Wales. Their implications for
the purposes of this chapter are that it is necessary to understand
benefices as part of the local worlds in which they are set, and as
varying in character according to the variation in what will be
termed a benefice's 'secular' characteristics. These characteristics
are not those of an exterior 'world' outside the benefice but those
of the locality of which the benefice is part.

Ranking the characteristics of benefices

The purpose of the following analysis is to explore the relationships between the attributes of the 549 benefices that were able
to respond to the 1989 survey. Table 4.1 lists the twenty-four
variables employed for analytical purposes and ranks them
according to the number of other variables with which strong or
medium statistically significant associations were found. The
columns opposite the variable list show the proportion of the
other twenty-three variables with which each was found to be
associated. The first column shows the proportion with strong
or medium associations, and the second the proportion with
strong, medium or weak associations; the third shows the
proportion of the other variables with which there was no association. The figures for each variable in the last two columns do
not total 100 because neither includes variables with which
there were very weak associations.

The 'rank order' is an order of *inference*. The higher a variable
is in the order, the more can be inferred from knowledge of a
benefice's position on that variable as to the benefice's position
on other variables. For example, knowledge of the size of a
benefice's population enables us to make inferences about the
position of the benefice on seventeen (74 per cent) of the other

variables. By contrast, knowledge of the proportion formed by revenue from collections of a benefice's income allows us to make inferences as to the benefice's position on only three (13 per cent) of the other variables.

Table 4.1   Associations between key benefice variables

Variables ranked in order of number of associations with other variables		% of possible associations which were		
		strong/ medium	strong/ medium/ weak	nil
population size	s	52	74	13
ecclesiastical classification	E	39	83	13
secular type	S	39	78	13
congregational size	e	39	74	22
benefice type		35	61	22
benefice income	e	35	57	22
density of population	s	35	56	35
number of Easter communicants (ECs)		26	56	26
number of parishes		26	39	43
number of 'lay workers'		26	56	35
miles travelled by incumbent		25	48	30
number of clergy in benefice		22	47	33
ECs as % of population		17	60	26
number of open Churches		13	65	26
lay commitment		9	35	30
lay participation		9	26	43
bilingualism		4	26	65
incumbent's years in benefice		4	13	83
ratio of confirmations to baptisms		0	35	57
% of expenditure on diocesan quota		0	30	44
language use in services		0	26	61
% expenses paid by benefice		0	17	56
% of income from collections		0	13	78
incumbent type		0	9	91

Note Associations are classified according to the values of the correlation coefficient: strong, .60–1.0; medium, .40–.59; weak, .10–.39. The *ecclesiastical classification* is designated by 'E' and its components by 'e'; *secular type* by 'S' and its components by 's'.

For the three main constructed variables used in the analysis –
secular type, the *ecclesiastical classification*, and *benefice type* – to be
of real value, it is important that they should rank highly in terms
of their power of inference. Indeed they do, the first two being
among those most frequently associated with the other variables,
as can be seen from the second column. These variables have
been designated by an 'E' for ecclesiastical and an 'S' for secular
respectively; each is made up of the variables indicated by 'e' and
's' respectively. Of the four variables in the top section of the
table, two are secular (population size and secular type) and the
other two are ecclesiastical (the ecclesiastical classification and
congregational size). This does not imply that the top two secular
characteristics directly affect the ecclesiastical characteristics in
the rest of the table. Rather, they do so indirectly through their
effect on the two most highly ranked Church characteristics. The
third key constructed variable – benefice type – also has a prominent position, ranking fifth in the order of inference.

Ecclesiastical and secular clusters

Now that an order based on the overall pattern of association has
been established, it is necessary to investigate which variables are
associated with which, discriminating between associations of
different strength. When we consider strong relationships only, it
is possible to discern two distinct clusters of variables, which we
shall term, respectively, 'ecclesiastical' and 'secular'.

The ecclesiastical cluster

The *ecclesiastical classification* involves distinguishing between
benefices primarily according to whether they are above or below
the median in respect of congregational size and benefice income
(see above, pp. 32–4). By definition, this classification must be
strongly related to a benefice's average number of communicants
(the measure of congregational size) and to the size of its income.
It was also found, however, to be strongly related to the number
of the benefice's Easter communicants. Because of the strong
relationships between these four variables, they will be referred to
as the 'ecclesiastical core'. There were no other variables which
were strongly associated with the four variables constituting the
core. The ecclesiastical core may be characterized as that part of

a wider ecclesiastical cluster that becomes apparent when only strong associations are considered.

The secular cluster

The only unambiguously secular benefice characteristics on which information was obtained were size of civil population and area; from these, population density is readily obtained. Population size and density were judged to be of primary significance for pastoral provision. The classification according to *secular type* derives from how benefices are jointly categorized on the two measures of size and density (p. 30–2). Naturally, secular type is strongly related to the two variables from which it is derived, and these three variables, between which the strongest relationships are found, constitute the 'secular core'. In this case, however, strong relationships do exist between the variables constituting it and other variables. The secular core plus four other variables constitutes the secular cluster. The ratio of ECs to population was strongly related to each of the three core variables. *Benefice type* was strongly related to both density and secular type (but not to population size). The number of parishes in a benefice and the miles travelled by the incumbent on a Sunday were found to be strongly related to density, and the number of parishes in a benefice was strongly related to benefice type, miles travelled and the number of open churches.

Benefice type distinguishes single- and multi-parish benefices, and the latter according to the viability of the parishes that they comprise. Since grouping of parishes is related to considerations of population size and density, the association of this variable with two of the secular variables (secular type and density), with the number of parishes and with the miles travelled on Sunday is not surprising. Benefice type is not, however, *strongly* related to the third secular variable (population size). What is of considerable importance is that the ratio of ECs to population is strongly related to all three of the secular variables but not strongly related to any of the ecclesiastical ones. Since the ratio expresses a relation between an ecclesiastical variable (ECs) and a secular one (population), it is to be expected that it will be related to both. In fact, the proportion formed by ECs of the population proves to be wholly a secular, and not an ecclesiastical, characteristic, having not even medium-strength relationships with the secular cluster.

The relation of this ratio to population is of this kind: the smaller the population of a benefice, the greater is the proportion of its population formed by ECs. It seems likely that these small benefices, where Anglican ECs form a relatively large proportion of the population, are the residue of an earlier, less secularized type of society where, though only a minority regularly attended a place of worship, the remainder were nominally Christian and attested to their allegiance by occasional conformity to the requirements of the established (Anglican) Church, which were that its members communicate at least three times a year, one of which had to be Easter.

To say that the ratio of ECs to population is not in this statistically identified sense an ecclesiastical variable is to say that it tells us little or nothing about the character of the life of the Church: it is not a measure of a benefice's success in bringing the members of a secular society into a relationship with the Anglican branch of the Christian community. Rather, it tells us something about the little society of which the Anglican congregation is part and in which the local church is set. It is an index of the secularization of that local society, a high ratio of ECs to population indicating a relatively low level of secularization. It is, however, necessary to stress that a relatively low level of secularization is still high in absolute terms. In this type of benefice ECs would still only form a mere one-seventh of the total population. That the ratio is as low as this even in small, predominantly rural, parishes is evidence of the extent of secularization of Welsh society as a whole.

Expanding the clusters

In defining the membership of the two clusters of variables, secular and ecclesiastical, we have, so far, considered only strong associations. When we consider both strong and medium relationships between variables, the picture becomes increasingly complex, since more variables come into play through the existence of associations of medium strength with some or all of the variables constituting the two clusters as previously defined.

The secular cluster
As far as the secular cluster is concerned, medium-strength relationships can be identified between benefice type and several

other variables: population size, the ratio of ECs to population, the number of churches and the miles travelled by the incumbent. With the additional evidence of these medium-strength associations it may be inferred that benefice type is related indirectly as well as directly to density via other density-sensitive variables.

The ecclesiastical cluster

Four new variables emerge in the ecclesiastical cluster. Two of these, the number of clergy and the number of 'lay workers', are each related positively to benefice income and to the number of ECs as well as to the ecclesiastical classification itself. The two other newcomers to the ecclesiastical cluster are the ratio of lay workers to average communicants, and the ratio of average communicants to ECs. The former is an index of active lay participation in parochial life and is termed the 'lay participation' ratio. The latter is effectively the proportion of all members (ECs) formed by those practising (average communicants) and may therefore be considered an index of 'lay commitment'. These two ratios were found to be related both to each other and to congregational size (average communicants).

With respect to the lay-participation ratio, the salient point is that the number of offices and functions that can be performed does not increase proportionally with increases in congregational size. In consequence, congregational size varies more than number of 'lay workers' and therefore is a greater determinant of variation in the ratio. Somewhat similar considerations explain the association between congregational size and the ratio of congregational size to ECs. Population affects both congregational size and the number of ECs. However, as established above, when a population is small the proportion of its members who are ECs is relatively high, but when the population is large the proportion of its members formed by ECs is lower. This diminishes the range of variation in ECs. However, no such factors appear to operate in the case of average communicants, variation in whose numbers is more directly proportional to variation in population size. While all three membership measures (ECs, average communicants, and lay workers) show medium-strength relationships with the size of benefice populations, the greater variability in average communicant numbers than in the numbers of lay workers or of ECs ensures that the variation in the two ratio measures (one of whose elements is average communicants) is associated with variations in the number of average communicants rather than with the other constituent of the ratio concerned.

Relations between clusters
The consideration of medium-strength relationships between variables not only brings in new variables and new relationships between core variables within each cluster; it also shows interconnections between the clusters. Relation-ships were found between population size in the secular cluster and number of clergy, number of lay workers and ECs in the ecclesiastical cluster. Relationships were also found between the ecclesiastical classification and its constituents (benefice income and congregation size) and the three variables in the secular core: population size, density, and secular type.

The size and density of a benefice's population, together with its degree of secularization, constitutes the situation with which the benefice has to cope. Different benefices address and respond to the same basic situation in different ways. In other words, the ecclesiastical world has a degree of autonomy from the demographic base which determines the range of responses but not the response itself. Hence it is possible to make stronger inferences between different types of ecclesiastical response (the variables in the ecclesiastical cluster) than between variables in different clusters. Weaker inferences can, however, be made between variables in the two different clusters because of the fact that the secular conditions the ecclesiastical.

However, the extent to which Church responses are conditioned by the secular world varies. The most strongly conditioned variables would appear to be those constituting the ecclesiastical core: namely, the ecclesiastical classification and its key constituents – congregational size and benefice income. The classification is a measure of advantage and is therefore positively related to the secular core: larger population sizes imply more human and financial resources, while high density reduces the costs of the delivery of services. As a result it is positively related to the number of available clergy and the number of lay workers. That these relationships are only of medium strength and only allow us to make weak inferences from the secular to the ecclesiastical is, however, evidence that congregational size and benefice income are not solely determined by secular factors.

An examination of the position of the ratio variables illustrates the complex and varying relationship between secular conditions and ecclesiastical response. We have seen that the ratio of ECs to population is essentially a secular variable: there are no strong or even medium relationships between it and any ecclesiastical variable. The implication is that the varying responses of benefices to their secular circumstances have little or no effect on this ratio. How could they? The ratio is the result of historical factors. A benefice can only affect this ratio by varying its number of ECs, since it cannot alter its population. A non-evangelistic benefice will have no effect on ECs; a successful evangelistic benefice will swell the ranks of the regular congregation and is likely to recruit new congregation members predominantly from occasional communicants: that is, from within the EC category. The chief result of evangelistic success will be that the number of the regular congregation will rise with only small effects on the total number of communicant members. Evangelistic success will thus be evidenced by a change in the ratio of congregation size to ECs, not in the ratio of ECs to population.

By contrast, the other two ratio measures so far considered (measuring lay commitment and lay participation) not only have no associations with any member of the secular cluster; they are unrelated to the (secularly conditioned) variables in the ecclesiastical core, with the necessary exception of the average number of communicants. Indeed, they have no other strong or medium associations at all. They stand, therefore, at the opposite pole from the other ratio (ECs to population), which is essentially determined by the secular variables, the core variables of the ecclesiatical cluster occupying an intermediate position between these two poles. The lay-participation and lay-commitment ratios would appear to be the product of action rather than structure. Sociologically they belong to the realm of human freedom rather than to that of necessity. Theologically, they are spiritually rather than socially determined. In managerial terms they are organizational 'success' measures.

It is important to note, however, that the two ratios are negatively related: congregations, of whose members a high proportion play an active part in parochial life (have high lay-participation scores) are likely to form a small part of the benefice's ECs (to have low average communicant-to-EC ratios). This is because

1   benefices with low populations have small congregations, and small congregations have relatively high lay-participation rates; and
2   in benefices with small populations ECs form a relatively high proportion of population, and average communicants a relatively low proportion of ECs: that is, such benefices have relatively low lay-commitment ratios.

There is, therefore, some relation between the lay-participation and lay-commitment ratio measures to secular factors after all, but it is a subtle one. Secular factors determine not the level of lay participation and commitment but the nature of the relationship between those levels.

So far we have omitted any reference to the last of the four ratio variables: the ratio of confirmations to baptisms. As discussed in Chapter 2, it cannot be viewed as more than a rough and ready indicator of the ability of a benefice to bring those who have been baptized to the bishop for confirmation. Its values proved to be negatively related to secular type in the sense that the more urban the benefice, the smaller the proportion formed by confirmations of baptisms. This is in the expected direction: the more urban a benefice, the greater the mobility of population, and the more difficult it is to exploit the evangelistic opportunity provided by baptisms. Interestingly, with respect to the ecclesiastical cluster the ratio is negatively related to benefice income while being positively related to congregational size. This suggests that high ratios of confirmations to baptisms are facilitated in benefices having small populations, but with larger congregations than might be expected given their population size. The implication is that if a benefice is more successful than the average one of its secular type in bringing the baptized to confirmation, this will have a positive effect on the size of its regular congregation. This variable would seem, therefore, to be primarily an ecclesiastical variable which is conditioned by secular factors: namely, the relatively low levels of geographical mobility associated with rural areas.

Benefices, secularization and mission in Wales

So far, evidence from the survey has been presented and analysed, and an attempt made to explain salient relationships which that analysis has revealed. To grasp the reality behind the evidence and analysis a further stage is required, that of interpretation. This chapter began by pointing up the distinction between 'church' and 'world' and argued that the latter term needs to be interpreted as something of which the Church is part rather than as that which constitutes its environment. However, statements about the secular world none the less specify the conditions under which the Church has to act. Our concern in this chapter has been with benefices: that is, we have focused on the local church as part of its local 'little society', whose characteristics constitute conditions of its action. Only through an examination of the Church–society relation across the full range of local contexts can one come to understand the functioning of the Church in Wales as a territorial organization.

We have already demonstrated, in our description of the dioceses in the previous chapter, the diversity of the Welsh province in both secular and ecclesiastical terms. The diversity of the six dioceses pales into insignificance when compared with the diversity of its 604 benefices, 549 of which supplied the data analysed here. In Chapter 2 the wide range of variation of individual benefice characteristics is displayed. However, to understand the relationship between the secular conditions under which the Church has to act and the results of those actions by the Church, it has been necessary to classify benefices in both ecclesiastical and secular terms and to examine the patterns of interdependence of the resultant variables. To say that our ecclesiastical variables are the results of action by the Church implies that they cannot be inferred from secular variables as they could be were ecclesiastical characteristics simply a religious 'response' to worldly 'stimuli'. It would, however, be remarkable if actions were not affected by the conditions of action.

The statistical analysis has shown quite clearly the existence of separate, interrelated clusters of secular and ecclesiastical variables with no strong relations between the clusters, thus demonstrating the relative autonomy of the religious from the secular. However, we did find medium-strength relations between the two clusters, which suggests a degree of similarity of Church action between benefices in similar secular circumstances – as is to be expected if action takes any account of the situation in which it is set. Of particular interest were the three chief ratio variables. Lay participation (proportion of regular congregation having some function or office) and lay commitment (proportion of all ECs formed by the regular congregation) had no strong or medium relationships with the secular cluster and were so related to only one ecclesiastical characteristic – average communicants. Hence lay participation and commitment appear to be the benefice characteristics least affected by secular characteristics – either directly, or indirectly through their effects on the core ecclesiastical variables. They are the result of relatively unconditioned action and hence genuine measures of spiritual success. By contrast, the ratio of ECs to population appears to be largely determined by secular factors. That particular ratio tends to increase as population size and density fall. Secular type which combines these measures provides a scale on the urban–rural continuum, low values implying 'rurality'. From this we have inferred that the above ratio tells us something about the local society of which a benefice's congregation is part. Effectively the ratio of ECs to population, while being a positive measure of occasional conformity, is an inverse measure of the degree of secularization of the locality.

We interpret this finding as follows. The data in this chapter which have demonstrated the diversity of the benefices of the Church in Wales in terms of quantitative measures conceal two qualitatively different social worlds. One is a remnant of the *old world* where everyone was nominally a Christian and attested to this by occasional conformity in the shape of attendance at the major festivals. The other is the *new world* where as much as one-third of the population (Jowell et al. 1988, 228) claims to have no religion; it is a world where citizenship and Christianity have ceased to be inseparable.

In the new world, the number of ECs is only slightly larger than that of average weekly communicants, and the two memberships rise and fall together. This is the world of high population-size/density benefices with above-median congregational sizes and incomes which is geographically associated mainly with the south-eastern seaboard and its hinterland: that is, with the archdeaconries of Newport and Llandaff, then, further west, with Margam and Gower, but also with Wrexham in the north-east.

The rest of Wales is characterized, apart from a few urban centres, by benefices with low population sizes and densities and below-median congregations and incomes. In this world the proportion of the population who receive Easter Communion, though not large, is larger than in the new world, and hence the number of ECs is higher than the relation between population and ECs in the new world would lead us to expect. The greater number of ECs in the old world is not matched by larger average weekly communicants, which means that the excess of ECs over what the new world would lead us to expect is the result of 'occasional conformity': that is, of attendance at major festivals only.

This interpretation of the results of the analysis is supported by other, previously unexplained, evidence provided by the Bible Society's census of Churches in Wales in 1982 (Brierley 1983), which concluded that, though numbers of ECs were falling, attendances in the Church in Wales were, at that time, rising. It is of interest to compare the census's figures for changes in attendances and membership for the Church in Wales by county with the ecclesiastical areas roughly approximating them. This comparison shows that the more urban the area, the better the fit between membership change and attendance change, which is what one would expect if it is correct to interpret our data concerning the ratio of ECs to population as a measure of the persistence of past social patterns involving low secularization and occasional conformity. If this interpretation is correct, the results of the census indicate that during the eighties there was a continuing secularization of the countryside, resulting in falling numbers of ECs (in Powys, Gwynedd and Dyfed) accompanied, however, in the case of Powys and Dyfed by an increase in congregational size.

Table 4.2 attempts to delineate the old and new worlds of Wales by classifying the Province's fourteen archdeaconries as 'old' or 'new' according to the EC-to-population ratios of their benefices (see also Map 2). The proportion of benefices in each archdeaconry having high ratios was calculated, and archdeaconries were ranked according to the size of this proportion. The results supplement the discussion of the characteristics of the archdeaconries in Chapter 3. While there are no surprises as far as membership of the 'old world' is concerned, what is notable, and not predictable, is how much 'older' Cardigan is than the other constituents of the 'old world'.

Table 4.2   The old world and the new: occasional conformity in the benefices of each archdeaconry (indicator: ratio of Easter Communicants to population; measure: percentage of benefices in top three deciles)

Diocese	Archdeaconry	%
The old world		
St Davids	Cardigan	70
Swansea & Brecon	Brecon	59
Bangor	Merioneth	59
St Davids	St Davids	53
St Asaph	Montgomery	50
Old and new		
Monmouth	Monmouth	41
Bangor	Bangor	32
St Asaph	Wrexham	30
St Asaph	St Asaph	30
The new world		
St Davids	Carmarthen	21
Swansea & Brecon	Gower	19
Llandaff	Llandaff	15
Monmouth	Newport	4
Llandaff	Margam	0

It is not surprising that archdeaconries in the north and south of Wales bordering on England should involve a mixture of the old and new worlds leading to middling levels of secularization. It might be expected, though, that Bangor would have relatively low levels of secularization and be in the 'old' rather than in the 'mixed' category. However, previous research has established that this archdeaconry is one where the Anglican Church is weakest in the sense of having fewer adherents compared with the other Christian denominations, and Bangor's relatively low ratio should be interpreted as reflecting the relative strength of Nonconformity in the area rather than a high level of secularization as such. It is surprising, given its intermediate position in

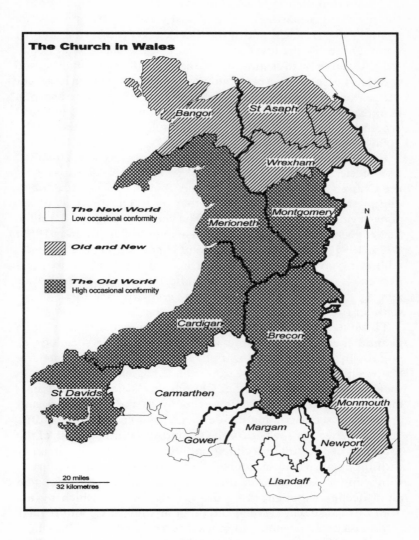

The Church in Wales

Bangor
St Asaph
Wrexham

The New World
Low occasional conformity

Old and New

The Old World
High occasional conformity

N

Merioneth
Montgomery

Cardigan
Brecon

St Davids
Carmarthen
Monmouth

Gower
Margam
Newport

Llandaff

20 miles
32 kilometres

terms of the secular type and ecclesiastical classifications, that the Carmarthen archdeaconry has such low ratios and therefore such a high level of secularization. However, it includes, in addition to the town of Carmarthen and the most western part of industrial south Wales (Llanelli and Burry Port), several erstwhile mining communities in the most western part of the south Wales coalfield, together with a number of other small towns and coastal resorts. These smaller communities tend to be neither large nor dense (i.e. not particularly urban) and not to have large and rich congregations (i.e. to be not particularly advantaged), but they are likely, because of their non-agricultural character, to be highly secularized.

In the last thirty years the Church in Wales has seen a marked and accelerating decline in the number of its ECs. This is seen by the Church as evidence of its decline: that is, of secularization in one of the sociological senses of that term. On the basis of the above evidence, this is a mistake. The various reports of the Bible Society censuses of religious attendance in Wales (Brierley 1983, 1985, 1991) show a patchy picture of change in religious activity, embracing growth, decline and stasis. While it is absurd to interpret these data optimistically, as indicating religious renewal or revival, they are inconsistent with the secularization thesis in the sense of the 'inevitable, continuous decline of religious practice'.

Those figures can be used to support the secularization thesis in another and arguably more fundamental sense. In sociology, as one might expect, 'secularization' refers primarily to something happening not to religious groups and religious practice but to society. The decline in the Church in Wales Easter Communicant figures is eloquent testimony to the continuous and progressive secularization of Welsh society. This process had its origins in the towns, where in the second and third quarters of the twentieth century ECs declined until they became more on a par with the regular congregation. The last quarter of the century is witnessing an extension of this process to the countryside. The rapid decline experienced by the Church in ECs which results from this cause will cease at the point at which ECs and regular communicants become identical throughout the Province. Variations in the number of ECs will, thereafter, cease to reflect the process of the secularization of society and become instead a measure of the extent of Anglican religious practice. In the terminology of the analysis used in this chapter, ECs will cease to be a *secular* and become an *ecclesiastical* variable – information which tells us something about 'the state of the Church' rather than about 'the state of society'.

Part Two

Beliefs, attitudes and activities

5

The activities and attitudes of clergy

In the second part of this study the focus of attention shifts from ecclesiastical units to people, first the clergy and then the active laity, the overall aim being to present a rounded view of the state of the Church. Of course, differing levels of analysis are complementary, and it will be important, for instance, to seek to understand the differing views of members of the Church, whether clerical or lay, by relating them to the variables of earlier chapters. A major initial concern is with the clergy's perception of the prospects for the Church, but necessarily that is bound up with the future of its ministry.

By the late 1970s the view was widely held that, as an occupation and a profession, the Anglican clergy were in crisis. That is a view which it is timely to reassess. In a study significantly titled *The Fate of The Anglican Clergy*, Towler and Coxon (1979, 194) argued that 'very soon the ministry will have dropped out of our occupational structure'. That study distinguished two types of clergy: those with a 'sectarian', world-rejecting orientation, and those who saw their role as witnessing and expressing their faith through service to the secular world. Similarly, Ranson, Bryman and Hinings describe Christian ministers in an increasingly rationalized society as being forced 'either to commit themselves to siege ... or undergo a reluctant metamorphosis and attempt to accommodate themselves to the modern rational form of things' (1977, 168). The latter orientation carried the implication that there was no distinctive role for the clergy within the Christian community. Perhaps for such reasons, some clergy left the ministry and moved into one or another of the 'helping and caring' professions. The 'siege' orientation presaged a ministry not to the local community but to a tiny band of adherents to an institution which had its origin in social conditions which no longer existed. Such a Church, being unable to recruit new members, was doomed to eventual extinction.

Since the 1970s, there has been little research work that enables us to evaluate the extent to which these dire predictions have been fulfilled. Attention has largely centred on issues to be faced by the Anglican Churches rather than any supposed crisis of their clergy. The perceived problems involve Anglican Church–State relations, declining membership, finance, social witness, the ordination of women, and moral issues, notably homosexuality. The situation of the parochial clergy has largely been approached obliquely, although the debate over the ordination of women as priests, now resolved in both England and Wales in favour of women's ordination, had earlier prompted studies of the position of women deacons (Aldridge 1987, 1989, 1992).

In a directly relevant way, however, concern over the financial position of the Church of England, brought about by its decline in membership during the 1980s, has made acute the problem of maintaining the ministry in rural areas and prompted a major report (ACORA 1990), which has drawn on studies by the Rural Church Project (Davies et al. 1990a, 1990b, 1990c, 1990d). The final report of that project (Davies et al. 1991) provides important information on the situation of the clergy in five rural dioceses in the Church of England and provides a basis for comparison with the data reported here concerning the clergy of the Church in Wales. As regards the attitudes of Welsh clergy, additional evidence is provided in a recent study by Jones and Francis (1998).

Although various issues have become salient at different times, what is clear is that longer-term changes in society have major implications for the role of the clergy. At the beginning of the century a Church of England parish priest enjoyed a high social status as the local representative of the established social order. He regarded his role as the care of all the inhabitants of his parish of any religion or of none, and not infrequently two-thirds of those inhabitants were at least nominally Anglican. The last seventy years have seen a decline not only in religious belief but also in respect for traditional authority. As a result, the Anglican clergy have lost their unquestioned role as leaders of the local community. They also face the task of carrying out their religious ministry to a population including many who are irreligious.

The data generated by this study make it possible to investigate the extent to which the 'clergy in crisis' diagnosis was correct. That diagnosis contains both general and particular elements. The general element is the hypothesis that secularization in its various forms inevitably leads to a crisis in the role of the clergy and a disintegration of the parochial system upon whose existence it is predicated. The more particular element concerns the Church of England. However, while there are similarities between the Church in Wales and its big sister church, as noted in Chapter 1, there are also differences. The organization of the Church of England at the parochial level has been characterized by a balance of power between the parish priest, acting as the deputy of the bishop and appointed by him or by a lay patron, and the parish council elected by an annual meeting of parishioners. However, at the time of the disestablishment of the Welsh Church, diocesan and provincial government of the Church of England was entirely in the hands of the clergy. As explained in Chapter 1, the Church in Wales adopted at its creation what was later to be called synodical government, thus constitutionally providing the laity with a far greater role not only than that afforded them in the Roman Catholic Church but also than that which they had hitherto enjoyed in the Church of England (Thompson 1970). This increase in the power of the laity was felt, however, chiefly at the higher levels of Church government; the parish priest continued to be the symbolic focus of 'the Church' in the view of most parishioners and, by virtue of his superior social and educational status, he predominated in the running of parochial life. Thus, the traditional role of the Welsh clergy at the parochial level was little disturbed by the changes brought about by disestablishment and remained in the early part of the century what it had been when the Church in Wales was still part of the Church of England.

The division between sectarian, world-rejecting, and secular, world-serving clergy noted by Towler and Coxon (1979) is not merely a reflection in the orientation of individuals of the difficulties of exercising the priestly role in a rapidly secularizing society; it is a manifestation of a wider organizational problem. That problem is how simultaneously to provide services to every member of the population of a given territory who already requires them, while at the same time deploying resources in such a way as to maximize effectiveness in winning new adherents.

Both Churches failed to face up to the problem, clearly analysed by the Paul Report on the Church of England (Paul 1964), of declining figures for ordinands and revenues in a rapidly changing but predominantly urban society, and strove to maintain the traditional territorial system, which required that each parish be served by a full-time ordained minister. Since this was no longer possible owing to the shortage of both men and money, parishes in rural areas were grouped, one clergyman serving several parishes. This change and the associated rapid fall in the numbers of clergy (above, Chapter 1) have major implications for the clergy role. Where rural parishes are grouped, the clergy become heavily dependent on the support of the laity simply to maintain the rudiments of traditional church life. In urban areas, where grouping is less frequent, clergy must become equally dependent on the laity if the local church is to exercise a missionary ministry. The result of declining clergy numbers must be that the ordained ministry becomes increasingly one ministry among other ministries within the Church, many of the other ministries being carried out by lay people. As well as accommodating himself to the loss of his unique ministerial status, therefore, the parish priest (now no longer necessarily a man) is required to reconcile within himself the often contradictory demands of pastoral care of the faithful and the evangelization of those outside the Christian Church. Further, like his Roman Catholic counterpart (see Hornsby-Smith 1987, 1989), he must mediate between laity and his ecclesiastical superiors. It might be expected, therefore, that clergy would experience considerable role conflict as well as status loss, leading to low morale and a tendency to hostility towards Church authorities, who would be perceived as the authors of these conflicting demands.

THE SURVEY OF CLERGY

There are two main sources of data for this chapter. In this section, data on clergy characteristics and attitudes derive from the survey of the 610 benefices, to which 549 incumbents and 138 other clergy responded. The questionnaire used in the survey comprised two main sections: one referring to the characteristics of benefices, and another focusing on the activities and attitudes of clergy themselves. The responses to the latter section are of central concern here. However, the description given in Part One of the benefices of the Church in Wales, deriving from the responses to the first part of the questionnaire, provides a background which is essential to interpreting the significance of data on the role and attitudes of clergy, since it furnishes detail about the very particular circumstances under which Welsh clergy work. In what follows, attention is mainly directed at incumbent clergy, but it is important sometimes to refer to the others, here termed *ancillary clergy*. The second source of information consists of reports submitted in 1991 by deanery chapters on discussions which took place among clergy on the basis of a discussion outline designed by the Board of Mission. This outline asked them to describe the secular setting of the Church in their deanery, and to evaluate its present position and prospects; the responses are particularly revealing as to the sources and nature of clergy attitudes.

The second section of the survey administered to incumbents and ancillaries comprised thirty-seven basic variables and provided information under the following headings: resources, professional history, perceptions of time-use, duties and needs, and attitudes towards the Church and the future. The questionnaire design enables, *inter alia*, subsequent analysis to reveal how far benefice characteristics are one source among others of variations in clergy activities and attitudes.

Congregations, services and clergy characteristics

What do the clergy and active laity do? They are much preoccupied with the maintenance of buildings and the raising of money. Apart from this, the efforts of the average congregation are largely devoted to maintaining the traditional pattern of services. The average incumbent conducts between three and four services every Sunday, and 16 per cent conduct five or more. One-third of incumbents travel more than ten miles to do so, and 11 per cent more than twenty miles. In spite of all this activity, however, 17 per cent of churches have no weekly service, and in many others the traditional pattern of services is maintained only by using lay persons to conduct them. The number of services is sometimes increased by the need to hold them in each of two languages. As Chapter 2 has noted, in just under two-thirds of the benefices, services are entirely in English for a congregation that is either monoglot English or includes only a small minority of Welsh speakers. In other circumstances, the official policy is for services to be bilingual; this is followed in 22 per cent of all benefices. In 15 per cent of all benefices, however, separate English and Welsh services are held, doubling the load on clergy which is usually already heavy since these benefices are frequently groups of parishes with several churches.

The median age of incumbents was fifty-two years. A tiny 1 per cent of them were under thirty, 18 per cent were in their thirties, 23 per cent were in their forties, 37 per cent were in their fifties, and 21 per cent were sixty or over. In respect of mobility, a salient figure is that 46 per cent had been in their present parish for less than five years: this suggests an average rate of movement of approximately one move every ten years. The proportions of clergy having experience outside their present dioceses, their dioceses of ordination and Wales are negatively related to the length of tenure of their present benefice and positively related to age. This pattern reflects the well-known Welsh version of what has been termed 'career spiralism'. This is the practice of moving geographically in order to move upwards socially. The Welsh version is that the last move, or a late move, in the sequence is to return to the starting-point, but at a higher level.

As regards ancillary clergy, a key point is their predominantly urban location: 61 per cent were in city benefices, and 82 per cent were in all urban benefices; a further 13 per cent were in the large, rural, nucleated-settlement category; only 6 per cent were in benefices which were 'small rural' or 'dispersed'. Also, 88 per cent were in 'large rich' benefices, while 77 per cent were in rectorial or single benefices; only 4 per cent were in 'non-viable grouped' benefices. In respect of differences between incumbents and ancillary clergy, it is notable that the latter tended to get a greater percentage of their expenses paid, but had lower earnings. Fewer ancillaries had Welsh-language capability and fewer had experience outside their present diocese, diocese of ordination or Wales. They took as many weekly services as incumbents, but fewer Sunday services. Because of their concentration in urban benefices, fewer ancillaries travelled many miles on Sunday to take services.

Perceptions of clergy activities

The respondents were asked to rank the nine activities on which they spent the most time and energy. They were presented with a list of seven differing primary activities. These activities are regarded as primary in the sense that they are activities which every incumbent must engage in by virtue of his office. Respondents were also given the opportunity to write in other activities which they ranked within their top nine. As Table 5.1 shows, the incumbents as a whole ranked visiting most highly, with over half of them putting it in first place. Two other items (conducting services, and study and sermon preparation) are virtually tied overall in second place, and a further pair (holding parish meetings and maintaining buildings) then follow, again having rather similar average rankings.

Table 5.1   Time and energy spent by clergy on various activities

Activity	*% ranking each activity 1–7*								Mean rank	Median rank
	1	2	3	4	5	6	7	TOTAL		
Visiting	51.9	22.5	11.2	7.7	4.5	1.3	0.8	99.9%	1.97	1
Services	13.9	20.0	28.1	16.8	10.9	8.3	1.9	99.9%	3.23	3
Study and sermon preparation	14.3	22.9	20.0	20.2	11.6	6.7	4.3	100.0%	3.29	3
Parish meetings	2.2	6.2	13.9	20.0	27.4	21.0	9.4	100.1%	4.65	5
Maintenance of fabric	5.5	8.8	8.3	14.3	20.9	20.6	21.6	100.0%	4.85	5
Travelling	3.1	9.5	8.1	10.8	13.0	20.8	34.7	100.0%	5.22	6
Other meetings	1.0	2.7	5.1	10.1	13.5	28.9	38.8	100.1%	5.74	6

The activity rankings of ancillary clergy were also obtained and could be compared with those of incumbents. Not surprisingly, given their concentration in urban benefices, they ranked travelling lower than incumbents, as they did time spent on the fabric of buildings, but services and parish meetings tended to be ranked higher. Since most ancillaries are assistant clergy and in the early stages of their careers, it is to be expected that public duties such as services and parish activities would rank highly.

However, the difference between ancillaries' first rankings and those of incumbents is greatest in the case of visiting. Therefore the time 'saved' by ancillary clergy on travel and care of the fabric tends to be devoted primarily to visiting rather than to services, study or meetings. This is a significant finding, because it suggests that most junior clergy are as 'traditional', if not more so, than incumbents.

It would be interesting to compare the pattern revealed by the survey with that found by Davies et al.'s (1991) study of rural parishes in the Church of England. However, that study groups sermon preparation with conducting services, whereas here it was grouped with private study, and it also groups all meetings and work concerning building maintenance under 'administration'. However, in both investigations the traditional and normative pattern of visiting, services and study quite clearly emerges.

In Wales, though, there were some notable variations on this pattern according to differences in parish type. Incumbents in single-parish benefices gave lower rankings to the holding of services than did incumbents in multi-parish benefices (a statistically significant difference; chi-square, $p<0.01$). Again, those in large rural dispersed benefices tended to rank services lower than others did, while those in small rural benefices, whether nucleated or dispersed, and in city benefices rated them higher (significant chi-square, $p<0.01$). In addition, the ranking accorded by incumbents to study and sermon preparation varied depending upon both secular and ecclesiastical features of the benefice. In sum, the more 'advantaged' the benefice, in the sense of being large, dense, rich, and single/rectorial, the greater the relative prominence of time spent in study (significant chi-square, $p<0.05$). This would seem to dispose of the essentially Victorian image of the busy urban incumbent, run off his feet, and the leisured rural parson devoting his time to natural history. These rankings point to rural clergy devoting, if anything, less time to study than their urban counterparts. A possible explanation, however, is that urban clergy have more time for study because they do less visiting: incumbents in benefices in all the rural categories of 'secular type' (see above, Table 2.1) ranked visiting more highly than did those with benefices in the urban categories.

Special study was made of the distinctive characterisics of those who did not rank visiting highly. There were in fact seventy-nine incumbents (14 per cent) who ranked at least three other activities higher than visiting. First, it transpired that they were markedly under-represented among incumbents who had been in post for less than five years. The implication is that visiting absorbs most time when the incumbent is getting to know a new benefice. A second, rather different, point to emerge was that those ranking visiting lower were more often to be found in benefices with high confirmation-to-baptism ratios. This may suggest that these individuals did indeed visit less than others and were ministering in benefices with stronger church traditions, so that they could cut down on general visiting, devoting themselves perhaps to those in trouble and distress. Alternatively, it may be that to rank visiting lower is not to do less of it, but to be more active than one's colleagues in other ways, perhaps even *in toto*.

There were also some distinctive patterns evident among Welsh-speaking incumbents. Altogether 34 per cent of respondents were able to preach in Welsh; these were included among 60 per cent who could take services in Welsh. Compared with other respondents, Welsh speakers ranked the taking of services significantly lower, but study and sermon preparation and also travelling were ranked significantly higher ($p<0.01$). This seems explicable in light of the fact that those able to preach in Welsh took rather fewer services than others did during the week (although not on Sundays) but were slightly older on average, and were more often in rural benefices.

The respondents were next offered five statements previously made by clergy about the running of their parishes and invited to indicate which one most closely conformed to their own experience. Of those responding (75 per cent), only 7 per cent opted for a description that characterized the parish situation as one in which the role of the laity was confined to meeting at intervals to hear what their priest had accomplished on their behalf. A further 22 per cent responded by drawing attention to the limitation of a small, mainly elderly congregation. An additional 14 per cent selected the 'nothing can happen without the vicar' pattern. Lay support was perhaps implied to be unsatisfactory in 43 per cent of cases therefore. On the other hand, 52 per cent opted for a characterization explicitly indicating good lay support, and a further 4 per cent implied as much, since they agreed with the statement that described the parish 'running itself'.

Satisfaction with the role

Three aspects of time pressure were probed in the questionnaire. The respondents were each requested to write in (a) something (one item) for which their life as a parish priest left hardly any time; they were also invited to consider what was required of a parish priest and then to write in (b) an item to which they devoted insufficient time and (c) a further item on which they had to spend too much time. It proved possible to use the same classificatory scheme for responses to (a) and (b); see Table 5.2.

Table 5.2   Time pressures on clergy

	Hardly time for (%)	*Insufficient time for (%)*
Personal		
Family life	26.2	3.9
Leisure	16.3	0.9
Hobbies	5.4	1.3
Relaxation	7.1	0.9
TOTAL	55.0	7.0
Clerical		
Spiritual activities	6.2	11.6
Study	21.7	30.0
Visiting	6.4	37.1
Other clerical activities	3.0	7.3
TOTAL	37.3	86.0
Other	2.8	2.8
None	4.9	4.2
OVERALL TOTAL	100.0% N=549	100.0% N=549

Under (a), a majority of 55 per cent identified personal items – most frequently family life and leisure activities – as being those for which they had hardly any time, while a further 37 per cent referred to aspects of the occupational role, the most prominent single item being study. Under (b), on the other hand, among their obligations as incumbents, 86 per cent of respondents identified occupational aspects as those to which they felt they devoted insufficient time – visiting and study being the items mentioned most often – with a further 7 per cent of respondents this time citing personal items. In summary, a majority of incumbents felt that some aspect of their personal life was being 'squeezed out' by the demands of their occupational role, but an even larger proportion felt that they were unable to devote sufficient time to one or more of their priestly duties. As regards (c), the professional responsibilities which took too much time were all 'profane'. Administration was the most prominent single item, being identified by 49 per cent of respondents, while 13 per cent referred to finance, and 12 per cent to care of the fabric of buildings. A further three items – the holding of meetings, travel and 'trivia' – were each mentioned by 5 per cent of incumbents. It is likely that the activities which were conceptualized as 'admin' and 'trivia' differed between respondents. These data show clearly that incumbents felt that they were distracted from what they conceived of as being core, sacred tasks by other tasks which were primarily instrumental or 'profane' in nature. This study shows, therefore, the Welsh Anglican clergy to be typical in this respect of Christian ministers of all denominations over a considerable period of time (see Blizzard 1956, 1985; Davies et al. 1991; Jud 1970; Lauer 1973; Ranson et al. 1977).

Of the activities cited by respondents for which they found hardly any time, the most frequently mentioned were family life and study. These are activities which take place in the clergy house and perhaps provide an indication of the extent to which clergy are visited as well as visit. In fact, almost two-thirds of respondents referred to items which bear witness less to the pressure imposed by the magnitude of clerical tasks than to that exerted by the social interaction in which they were involved, which intruded on various legitimate claims on their private space. Here more important than the distinction between the sacred and the profane components of their role is that between the public and the private (Freytag 1965, 62).

Satisfaction and dissatisfaction with the clergy role were explored more generally by asking respondents to indicate the most rewarding and most frustrating aspects of their life as parish clergy. On the positive side, some facet of contact with people was most often referred to (by 22 per cent), but this was nicely balanced by the most frequently cited (by 17 per cent) source of frustration: 'people's failings'. The other rewarding aspects indicated by 10 per cent or more of incumbents were pastoral care

(16 per cent), the services they provided (14 per cent), the help of the needy (11 per cent), and contact with youth (10 per cent). Correspondingly, on the negative side were administration (16 per cent), elements of the clergy role definition (13 per cent), insufficiency of resources (13 per cent), and excessive time devoted to travel (11 per cent).

The pattern of responses did not fall easily into Davies et al.'s (1991) classification of the replies by their English rural respondents to job-satisfaction questions. Those authors distinguished between satisfaction arising from ministry to individuals, from the worship of God, and from ministry to the community. However, the Welsh respondents clearly favoured interaction with individuals (ranked highest by Davies et al.'s respondents), and, like the English, 'none identified administrative or organizational tasks as specific sources of satisfaction' (Davies et al. 1991, 92). Hence, there is confirmation of the picture presented so far but with the addition of some new concerns. The strong pastoral orientation is evident, as is the irritation at time spent on the profane activity of administration. Issues of role definition often centred on the division of responsibilities between the clergy and the laity. To this are added resource problems and a specific concern with the amount of time taken up with travelling.

Attitudes to the future

The clergy-attitude section of the questionnaire concluded with four questions which invited each respondent to look towards the future and identify (a) the greatest cause for hope and (b) the greatest source of temptation to despair – first in respect of the religious situation in Wales, and secondly in relation to the Church in Wales itself (Tables 5.3 and 5.4).

In addition to spiritual reasons for hope, both institutional and populational reasons were cited. At the institutional level, cause for hope was found in Wales through the ecumenical movement, and in the Church itself through 'leadership'. At the populational level, hope lay particularly in the increased involvement of young people in religion in Wales and of lay people in the Church in Wales. On the other hand, incumbents were tempted to despair in respect of religion in Wales because of failings at the institutional level and the uncooperativeness or conservatism of people.

Table 5.3   Causes for hope

Religious situation in Wales		Church in Wales	
	%		%
Religious unity	25.9	Increased lay support	23.5
Spiritual outlook	20.5	Spiritual support	17.3
Involvement of young	12.4	Leadership	12.5
'People'	10.4	Willing change	6.8
Religious renewal	7.9	Unity	6.3
Evangelism	4.6	Evangelism	6.3
Leadership and structure	3.1	Renewal	6.1
Increase in ordinands	0.6	Increase in ordinands	4.0
Others	13.0	Ordination of women	1.9
None	1.7	Others	15.2
TOTAL	100.0% N=549		99.9% N=549

Table 5.4   Temptations to despair

Religious situation in Wales		Church in Wales	
	%		%
Disunity	17.7	Church structure	20.8
People's failings	15.1	Lack of spirituality	16.7
Church structures	14.1	Conservatism	16.3
Conservatism	13.9	Divisiveness	14.0
Adverse change	7.8	Too few clergy	6.8
Membership level	7.4	Resource problems	6.0
Secularism	6.0	Concern, not despair	5.4
Concern, not despair	5.4	Adverse change	4.7
Low spirituality	4.6	Women not priests	2.7
Others	7.8	Others	6.6
TOTAL	99.8% N=549		100.0% N=549

In relation to the Church itself, its own structure is the major problem, and to the conservatism of people was added what respondents seemed to see as the general 'spiritual climate'. Jones and Francis (1998) report similar criticisms by Welsh clergy of existing Church structures, together with complaints about an overall mood of conservatism.

These clergy reactions to their own Church have given the

Church authorities food for thought. That Church in Wales structures are a prominent item giving rise to despair must be worrying, particularly given that Church leadership as a cause for hope is mentioned rather less often; also, despair at divisiveness is more evident than hope in respect of unity. On the other hand, the outlook on lay support within the Church seems positive, but with a certain qualification. Further exploration of the patterns of clergy response in relation to spirituality suggests that, at root, the enthusiasm of the active laity for the associational life of the Church only emphasizes for some respondents the lack of that spirituality which should give these activities their purpose and meaning. So 'lack of spirituality' is more prominent in the 'Church' than in the 'Wales' responses because it is a reaction to lay support for the Church which these clergy do not experience in the 'Wales' context.

There was a particularly marked association between sources of temptation to despair in relation to the religious situation in Wales and the incumbent's age. Those under forty emphasized conservatism and 'people's failings'; those between forty and fifty, Church structures; those between fifty and sixty, disunity; and those over sixty, falling membership, secularism and undesirable change. It is not hard to see these differences as a reflection of the concerns of successive generations, rather than as simply the reaction of different age-groups to the contemporary situation.

Cross-tabulating these four general attitude variables yields six relationships, four of which proved to be statistically significant. The relationship between respondents' causes for hope in the Church in Wales and for temptations to despair regarding the religious situation in Wales was not significant; nor was that between causes for hope in Wales and temptations to despair about the Church. The strongest associations were between responses to the two 'hope' questions and the two 'despair' questions (each significant chi-square, $p < 0.001$). Weaker relationships were found between hope and despair in Wales and also between hope and despair in the Church (each significant chi-square, $p < 0.05$). The distinction made by clergy between the religious situation in Wales and the state of the Church in Wales was therefore weaker than that between 'hope' and 'despair'. This suggests a tendency among some respondents to identify the religious situation in Wales with that of their own Church, and thus a failure to recognize the ecumenical dimension in the questions asked about Wales.

In sum, the responses to the attitudinal section of the questionnaire are at best mixed in terms of their implications for the future. It is not just the 'spiritual climate' that gives cause for concern but also Church structures themselves. Also, any tendency for clergy to see the missionary situation in Wales in predominantly or exclusively Anglican terms does not bode well for its future evangelistic effectiveness. Having adumbrated some key themes on the basis of survey data, we can usefully cross-reference and deepen our understanding of context by proceeding to the reports from meetings of the clergy in each deanery.

THE CLERGY IN THE DEANERY

As indicated above, clergy were asked to discuss and report back on various topics pertaining to the life of the Church and its future. The responses take in comments on the secular setting of the Church, issues to do with hierarchical relations, parochial organization and resourcing, as well as spiritual concerns. Sixty-two (or 77 per cent) of the deaneries responded to this part of the wider inquiry.

The implications of the secular world

Particularly useful as context for clergy attitudes is information on the secular world in which the Church in each deanery is set. Just what were the salient aspects of the environment within which clergy were working? *Population growth* was mentioned by five deaneries in urban dioceses, while *commuting* was highlighted as a concern in nine deaneries in urban dioceses, and in three in rural ones. In the south-east of Wales population growth and commuting are clearly connected, while in north Wales commuting is associated with the north-east borders. Commuting appears to have a double pastoral significance. It makes for rapid population growth in favoured areas, and it also leads to privatized lifestyles, since exhausted drivers want to do little on their return except nod off in front of the television. This means that they are unwilling to take part in Church activities. It is also seen as putting marriages under some strain.

In-migrants, by contrast, are seen as a major concern in the rural dioceses. This is, of course, partly a difference in terminology, but also one in reality, since in-migrants in the rural dioceses are associated with declining natural populations. Fourteen deaneries, again predominantly in rural dioceses, mentioned the *loss of young people*. The link here is evident, although clergy themselves implied it directly only in a minority of cases, that the homes that could have been taken by the young are being taken over by outsiders. Another popular and related rural theme was the *growth of the elderly population*. One factor which can be associated with the out-migration of young people and the growth of the elderly population is the *decline in farming*, mentioned by six deaneries in rural dioceses.

Unemployment was mentioned by 40 per cent of deaneries in the more rural dioceses and by 26 per cent of deaneries in the more urban dioceses. Thus unemployment emerges as not simply an urban problem but also a widespread phenomenon in rural Wales, and one well recognized by clergy. A further concern, the *Welsh language*, was mentioned in various contexts by eighteen deaneries, mainly in north and west Wales. This suggests that rather little recognition is given by clergy to the problems of ministering to Welsh-speaking people in urban areas of south Wales where they form a minority, but one whose numbers are none the less significant since such areas have large total populations.

Turning next to the implications of the secular world for the Church, seven deaneries drew attention to problems for ministry posed by secularization. That most of these were in rural dioceses is suggestive of a notion highlighted by the evidence of Chapter 4 that rural areas were currently undergoing a process of secularization which had long ago come to pass in more urban areas. In reacting to this situation – that is, in framing responses to life in a 'post-Christian' society – one can note that two polar positions are possible. One can regard the Christian community as a few gathered out of the world, and the Church as an ark buffeted by a sea of secularity, or one can view the world as the object of the Church's mission. It is significant, therefore, that in what was defined as a decade of evangelism only around a quarter of deaneries chose to specify mission/evangelism. Indeed, particularly revealing is the point that the problems of proclaiming the Gospel were mentioned so infrequently in reports concerning the life of the Church and its future. However, some of those not highlighting mission, perhaps because of its 'evangelical' flavour, did mention the need for the Church to witness through service. Ten deaneries picked up this last theme, but only four of these also stressed mission, thus confirming the view that these tend to be seen as alternatives. Also, one must note that mission implies a need to go where people are: to do the modern equivalent of getting up and preaching in the marketplace. This is difficult today given the privatized nature of so many lives, a phenomenon also referred to as 'loss of community', itself associated with secularization. That this issue is only mentioned in one report may signify a wider tendency of ministry to be personal, and the loss of the traditional role of clergy as community leaders and of any conception of their ministry as the service of the community as well as of individuals.

Central to the problem of evangelism is the laity. Given the clergy-to-people ratio in most deaneries, the clergy can scarcely preach the Gospel to the world on their own. Over one-third of reports mentioned the lay ministry as being important and in some way problematic. In this connection it is, of course, of the essence that the laity are collectively 'in' the world in a way which no single incumbent can be and that they act, therefore, as a bridge between the clergy and the world. However, it is no good having a willing and non-'conservative' laity if they are not equipped to witness. Eleven deaneries mentioned the need for *better instruction for the laity*. An important consequence of secularization is that many people are totally ignorant of the Gospel to the extent of not knowing what happened at Christmas and Easter, and though the lay Church members are not that ignorant, they require far more instruction than in pre-secular days. Consequently, twelve deaneries mentioned the importance of teaching: the Church must become a teaching Church as well as a preaching Church. A similar number referred to the importance of evangelism and education specifically among *young people*. A basic problem is the decline of the village school, within which the local parish had a traditional role, and the decline of *Church schools* in particular. However, this last important aspect of the Church's witness was mentioned relatively infrequently.

Also mentioned, but again infrequently, was the role of the *occasional offices* such as baptism, marriage and burial. These might have been referred to either as an opportunity to make contact with the unchurched or as a problem: the use of the church as an up-market Register Office. Whichever view is taken, these offices provide an important link or 'interface' between the Church and secular society. Only four deaneries referred to this issue, and then only with reference to baptisms.

Hierarchy and the deanery

Turning next to issues internal to the Church, it becomes apparent that all is not well with hierarchical relations. As many as one-half of the reports contain at least implied criticism of ecclesiastical administrators. The parochial clergy feel that they are the Church in the institutional sense, that 'the buck stops with them', and that they can reasonably look to their superiors for help and support. However, they find the emphasis in the relationship is on the upward flow of information, with clergy engaged in form-filling or providing answers in the context of visitations, while their superiors rarely substantively assist but instead engage in high-level meetings or generate slogans, such as 'mutual responsibility' or 'the decade of evangelism'. Etymologically, hierarchy is rule by priests, and many of these priests feel ruled without there being genuine participatory consultation. It is apparent therefore that there is a degree of alienation of the parochial clergy from central bodies and Church leaders.

On a more positive note, it does, however, appear that clergy saw the deanery itself as having a continuing role in Church life – especially so in rural areas – and that, in an identifiable sense, deanery clergy think in deanery terms. In only four cases did deaneries lack any sense of themselves as a unit, although as many as a quarter felt that, as at present defined, their deanery was not a natural unit. It would not appear, therefore, that deanery areas are generally unsuited to modern conditions, but variations between deaneries give some grounds for concern. Although it was felt that the active agents of mission were and must remain the parishes, several respondents saw the deanery as having a major facilitating role in that connection.

Deaneries may be classified into various urban and rural types, with their somewhat differing needs. Though deaneries in rural dioceses tend to have fewer clergy than deaneries in urban dioceses, the average difference is not great. However, the variations in the ratios of people to clergy between individual deaneries do seem excessive, there being a ratio of over 10,000 in Caerphilly and more than 8,000 in Merthyr, Mold and Pontypool, while at the other extreme the ratios in Llanfyllin and Edernion are 714 and 800 respectively. Even when the very real problems of ministry to rural areas are taken into account, this gap seems hard to justify.

The Church in the deanery

A further topic considered by deaneries was the parochial organization and resourcing of the Church. In this connection it is clear that, in spite of the substantial fall in clergy power in the thirty years preceding the inquiry, this was not perceived by the main body of responding deaneries as having created insuperable problems, and this fact is undoubtedly related to the growth in lay activity over the same period. This is not to say that in some deaneries the parish system is not always near collapse through lack of clergy (e.g. because parishes have been grouped 'up to the hilt'), or that there are not major problems in filling benefices in some areas, especially with appropriately qualified clergy. It is merely to claim that the majority of deaneries did not experience clergy shortage as a major problem.

What is, however, felt to be a central problem is that the Church has *too many buildings*. The issue of buildings was mentioned by well over half the deaneries, twenty-eight saying that they had too many. Four deaneries thought the number of their buildings was about right, and one complained about the cost of renovation. However, some reports made clear that the problem is not merely one of excess. The buildings concerned are frequently in the wrong place, unsuitable for modern use and expensive to maintain and run. There is no doubt that generally deaneries feel that an enormous amount of clergy and lay resources is devoted to the maintenance of unnecessary and/or unsuitable buildings and that this is a great impediment to the work of the Church however that is conceived.

Naturally connected is the issue of *money*. Twelve deaneries out of thirty-five in the more rural dioceses mentioned money as a problem, while only two out of the twenty-seven in the more urban dioceses did so. Of those mentioning money, only three complained about the diocesan quota, and only two the lack of lay giving. This is a rather different picture from that forthcoming when clergy are asked about those aspects of their vocation that they find most burdensome, for then the amount of time spent on such activities as fund-raising, administration and maintaining buildings ranks high (see above, this Chapter). The picture presented by this part of the inquiry largely reflects the actual position with regard to money revealed by the statistics concerning parochial finance, which is not unsatisfactory for maintaining the present pastoral structure. What *is* unsatisfactory is how much money is absorbed in the maintenance of buildings.

That being said, in some deaneries resources are insufficient even in relation to pastoral structure, and it might be expected that these deaneries would favour the solution provided by a *deanery team ministry*. Only five of the sixty-two responding deaneries indicated this solution, but under-resourced deaneries are likely to be over-represented among those who did not respond. Only one of these five was a deanery in a rural area, and, taken together, they had high people-to-clergy ratios and relatively large populations. The rural deanery emphasized the burden placed on clergy by having to minister to a large area rather than a small population. In the other three deaneries various reasons were given for operating different sorts of team ministry. These were the need for clergy to develop and exercise specialist skills; the need to serve an area which had a unity of the kind that the traditional parish once exhibited but which was to be found, in an urban area, only at the deanery rather than at parish level; and, lastly (most elaborately), the need in a very large urban deanery for several team ministries based on different centres in the same deanery, and including lay people as well as clergy. A benefit of the latter was felt to be that clergy would be appointed to fulfil a function in a ministerial team rather than enter into a 'monogamous marriage' with a parish; each parish would have a variety of clergy available to it, and each clergyman a wider field in which to exercise his ministry. These contrasting responses demonstrate just how flexible the concept of team

ministry is and how it can be adapted to widely differing circumstances.

There is some evidence to suggest that rural deaneries see new
structures and forms of organization as by definition 'urban' and
ipso facto unsuitable. As one deanery reported:

> In recent years there has been an attempt to take town thinking about
> the norms for a church and impose them on rural areas. However they
> should be seen as different expressions of the presence of Christ in His
> world. A tangerine is not a failed orange.

The point should be well taken. However, its converse is also
true; urban parishes have for the last 150 years been haunted by
the traditional norms of the parochial system in a predominantly
rural society, which are inapplicable in many urban settings: a
fact of life of such antiquity in urban deaneries that it is taken for
granted. None the less an urban parish need not be viewed as a
failed rural 'tangerine'.

Given the timing of this inquiry, when consultations were
taking place within the Church about the *ordination of women*, this
topic might have been expected to attract frequent mentions.
Lack of women priests for some, feared disunity for others, might
have been expected to occur regularly in the section of the reports
concerned with the future of the Church. In fact it did not, only
four deaneries mentioning the issue. It was also to be expected
that some reference, positive or negative, would be made to the
charismatic movement. In fact it was mentioned only once. It is
undeniable, therefore, that the reports exhibited a relative lack of
concern for topical issues, a state of affairs obliquely recognized
by one deanery which reported that its clergy 'recognized the
need to move into the 20th [*sic*] century'!

The deaneries were asked about *ecumenical relations* and of the
forty-five that responded the vast majority reported good relationships with other denominations. Just two deaneries said they
had no relationship with other denominations, and two had no
other denominations locally with which to have relationships.
However, in nearly every case existing relationships were
extremely limited. Though the 'bitterness and hostility' between
the Anglican Church and the Free Church denominations so
characteristic of the nineteenth and early twentieth centuries still
exists, it is clearly very limited in its incidence but has not been

replaced by any positive co-operation. This is partly due to the very weak state of Nonconformist denominations in many areas, but even when this was not the case, the Christian denominations were very far indeed from being 'united in mission', and only four deaneries specified improving co-operation as one of their aims.

Spiritual concerns

So far this analysis has omitted any mention of the things felt by clergy to be most central to the life of the Church: namely, prayer and worship. In this connection it must first be noted that *religious language* permeates the reports. Writers routinely referred to the importance of 'taking the Gospel seriously', 'following the example of Our Lord', etc., at appropriate points in their reports and frequently concluded with some statement about the Gospel or the wider conception of the Church, or God's purposes. Secondly, it is significant that clergy had been given the opportunity to raise substantive 'spiritual' issues within a broader framework so that it could be seen which ones they *did* raise. Given this context, the main topic to emerge was *the centrality and importance of worship in the life of the Church*. The clergy were in this respect concerned not with form but with content, not with the manner of expression but with what was expressed. Worship should be the expression of the gifts of the Spirit: love, peace, joy and, in the Eucharist, thanksgiving. If worship was not this, then something was wrong with the spiritual life of worshippers. This type of response was not unexpected, but it has important links to an underlying dilemma of the Church involving communication and the manner of expression.

An important form of Christian communication and witness is through the *liturgy*, mentioned in eighteen reports, five times favourably and thirteen times unfavourably. The main view expressed was that the present liturgy is, in the words of one report, 'suspended uneasily between the past and the present'. A more extreme view ran as follows: 'Can one justify the mock-Tudor, quasi-Laudian English of the 1984 Prayer Book? The lamentable poetry of the collects, the poor variety of prefaces, the rigid single Canon, the lack of imaginative alternatives, all serve to mar Church life.'

A further point made by this writer, and shared with many

other deanery reports, concerns the repetitive and limited nature of the readings prescribed by the lectionary. The general consensus among the thirteen reports commenting unfavourably is that the present liturgy is inadequate both pastorally and evangelically. Jones and Francis (1998) similarly report discontent among their sample of younger Welsh clergy with the traditionalism of the authorized liturgy.

Despite the near-absence of mention of the charismatic movement, there is an underlying concern in connection with liturgy and in other respects with issues which that movement has sought to address. One deanery report quoted the remark of a clergyman: 'The Church has gone cold.' Charismatics, by contrast, are 'hot' – filled with the fire of the Holy Spirit. It is clear from the responses that, however good the state of the Church in Wales, it is not ablaze. Worship, however dignified and well conducted, however relevant to the lives of worshippers and vital to their spiritual health and growth, is not, in the words of one report, 'a celebration', an outpouring of joy; and because it is not, it may be less attractive to outsiders.

The dilemma that the Church faces can be highlighted by referring back to the concern of clergy with improving teaching. An initial question is not how the Church presents the faith to the outside world, but how it presents the faith to its own people. Is the faith presented to Christian people as the Gospel, as the 'good news' of Jesus Christ, news so good and so exciting that they want to rush out and tell everyone about it? If not, how is the faith to be presented and received in churches? There is a long-established tradition in Anglicanism, which says in effect: the world is a very nasty and evil place, and life is full of sufferings and troubles and would be unsupportable but for the consolations of religion. This seems to smack of bad news as much as good. Or the good news is not very good: there is a drug to diminish the pain.

'For the most part', reads one report, 'the parishes in the deanery are ... preoccupied with maintenance rather than mission, more anxious about survival rather than revival.' It then goes on: 'In far too many cases direct financial contributions are far from being realistic and certainly not sacrificial.' This response is suggestive of the notion that in so far as clergy feel that consolation is not what the Gospel is about, then they want people to be challenged to sacrifice, to give up things, their money, their 'own' vicar, their traditional habits and customs. Several reports affirm the centrality of the Cross in Christian teaching, but to refer simply to the Cross, to the need for discipline, sacrifice, and self-denial, makes Christianity into a religion of moral effort, a burden imposed, a duty to be discharged, an ascetic ethical code. Against this, some Christians assert that what comes first is the 'experience of the living Lord – risen, ascended, triumphant ... The Gospel is good news, not bad news, even though accepting it requires accepting that the triumph is won through a suffering which Christians are called to share. It is a message of hope.' Evidently, the implicit debate within the Church reaches beyond expressive style to the basic theology itself.

TRADITION AND A NEED FOR CHANGE

The data from the two sources of information about the clergy are in broad harmony. The evidence from the survey bears witness to the overwhelmingly traditional role definition of Anglican clergy, wedded as they are to the activities of visiting, study and the conducting of services. From the responses of the deaneries, one infers an awareness of problems, but perhaps insufficiently of opportunities. None of the problems is seen as insuperable, including even the fall in clergy numbers, but nor do the clergy come across as being particularly 'pro-active'. There was widespread recognition of the significance of demographic change; also of problems posed for the ministry by what may be understood as aspects of secularization. However, only a clear minority pointed up the importance of mission/evangelism. It was also notable that clergy seemed rather conscious of problematical aspects of the lay ministry, there being said to be a need for better instruction. Mentioned, but not notably stressed, was the need for evangelism among young people and, associated with this, religious education. A lack of dynamism is suggested by the fact that, although the occasional offices were referred to, they were hardly highlighted as a possible bridgehead into secular society.

Particularly problematical, however, are hierarchical relations: there is evidence of alienation from ecclesiastical authorities.

However, deanery organization is viewed as having a continuing and creative role in Church life. The worst resource problems concern buildings: there are either too many of them and/or they are awkwardly situated or unsuitable for modern use; certainly too much clergy and lay time is devoted to the maintenance of unnecessary or unsuitable buildings. The deaneries reported on the whole good ecumenical relations, but it could be inferred that generally these relationships were extremely limited. A lack of dynamism is again suggested by the near-absence of references to the challenge posed by the charismatic movement, although a significant minority is conscious of problems with the present liturgy.

It is now possible to relate these conclusions to the diagnosis made by Towler and Coxon (1979) concerning the crisis of the Anglican clergy. As Davies et al.'s study of rural England concluded:

> Our findings demonstrate that post mortems for the parochial ministry are premature. The content and meaning of clergy work remains firmly within traditional understandings of the parochial ministry and of the parson as the focus of that ministry.   (Davies et al. 1991, 102)

Likewise the clergy of the Church in Wales are not currently in a state of crisis: it is, rather, the Church that is experiencing a time of difficulty and challenge, and these two facts are closely related. All the factors which were supposed to lead to clergy crisis are present but have been accommodated by clergy through a return to, and a re-emphasis on, the distinctive characteristics of the traditional clergy role. By distinguishing the sacred and profane elements within that role, clergy have been able to accommodate the increased lay participation which is functionally necessary at the parochial level. This distinction is, however, dysfunctional for the Church as a whole, which requires for its survival an emphasis on a sharing of the whole ministry of the Church, both pastoral and evangelistic, between clergy and laity – something which is well understood by Church leaders. This produces a degree of estrangement between parochial clergy and the Church hierarchy (see also Harris 1969). The absence of such sharing produces a further decline in resources. This increases pressures on the parochial clergy which intensify their division between the sacred and secular and their exclusive emphasis on the sacred elements of the traditional clergy role. This in turn makes the redefinition of that role even more difficult.

Paradoxically, this state of affairs has come about not because of a lack of resources but because of their availability. The existence of central wealth has enabled barely viable benefices to remain in existence and thus created a situation in which participants are fully absorbed in the struggle to contribute to clergy salaries and maintain buildings, to the detriment of the currently vital task of evangelism.

6

The lay view from the parish

In this chapter we commence a consideration of lay attitudes within the Church in Wales. There follows in Chapter 7 an exploration of the social characteristics of the laity, and further exploration of their attitudes, both religious and secular. It must be stressed that the focus is on individuals who are, to some extent at least, religiously active within their parishes on a regular basis, in terms of their participation in services, meetings and other events and initiatives within church life; they are to be distinguished from those who merely have some nominal identification or intermittent acquaintance with Anglicanism (perhaps via the occasional offices). That these members of the community are strategically vital is readily demonstrated when one recalls the scale of the evangelical task facing the Church, there being approximately forty-seven individuals in the target population for each active church member.

The difference between the approach taken towards the laity in this chapter and the next is, at one level, one of method: here the content of reports from parish councils of discussions of a set of issues concerning the life of the contemporary Church is considered, while in Chapter 7 the data being analysed derive from a survey of the laity. Thus, as in Chapter 5, insight into group life is usefully complemented by aggregated information on individuals. However, going beyond this, the nature of the groups whose views are here being considered is vital: those within the parish council are participating in operative working groups within the Church, in part creating their own agendas, and acting responsibly to establish common ground and a joint stance on issues and problems. Just as was the case for the clergy within the deanery (Chapter 5), these groups are attempting to define and react to issues and problems in a religiously meaningful way, the activity in which they are engaged being an essential moment within the life of the Church. By contrast, there is a certain artificiality about individuals' responses to surveys, such as the survey of the laity reported in Chapter 7, necessary though it is for information to be collected in this way in modern conditions.

The topics the parishes were invited to discuss raised religious and organizational issues, which respectively give rise to moral and to technical considerations. If the Church is, theologically, the 'Body of Christ', then it is so in reality only if the consciousness of the active laity is informed by the Christian world view, and their activities form part of an effective organization. For instance, if those in parish councils fail to understand religious concepts and issues, what hope is there for the relatively ignorant unchurched? It is for this reason that we shall have occasion below to critique, from an Anglican theological point of view, some of the opinions expressed. On the other hand, since the parishes constitute the Church, it is their effectiveness as organizational units that counts, for without them there would be nothing for the Church hierarchy to do. No doubt organizational issues – concerning, for instance, money and buildings – are addressed by parish councils with varying degrees of effectiveness. The essential point is that, while achievements and failures at this level are conditioned by the character of the organizational structure to which they belong, they in part determine it.

At this point it is important to clarify further the meaning of the key term of this chapter and the next. 'The laity' here being investigated is broadly to be understood as the 'faithful' members of the Church: that is, those who attend regularly Sunday by Sunday. However, to increase understanding there is a need not just to be reminded how this key term is used in ordinary parlance but also to specify more exactly how this category is viewed within the Church itself. In this connection the key idea is that the Church is itself the *laos* (the people) of God: it is itself a community of worshipping believers, and local Churches are its manifestations. The *laos* is emphatically not to be confused with the ordained ministry (a profession). Nor is the parish priest inferior in kind to his organizational superior the bishop: they are both priests, and both represent the wider church to the local church, and vice versa. They are set apart from the rest of the *laos*, have a 'sacred' character, because they represent the whole. The term 'laity' in English is used restrictively to refer to those who are not ordained, a use that arose out of what Anglicans see as a medieval corruption of the orthodox doctrine of the Church, which identified it with priesthood, as exemplified by the usage he 'went into the Church' meaning 'was ordained'.

For this reason the laity cannot be conceptualized as 'lower participants', workers, or public, since they form a constitutive element of the community under study, differing from the clergy only in their lack of representative function. A key part of this study involves an attempt to understand the conceptual worlds of the laity in order to evaluate the prospects and possibilities for the Church. For instance, what chance is there of changing the direction of the Church's activities (as sought by its leadership) 'from maintenance to mission'? That is bound to depend crucially on lay attitudes.

The parochial church councils (PCCs) of a sample of parishes were each asked to hold and report on discussions of seven topics indicated in an outline (devised by the Board of Mission). The selected parishes were geographically representative of the Church in Wales, being chosen by the rural dean of each deanery. Altogether responses were received in 1991 from seventy-two parishes in sixty-seven out of the seventy-seven deaneries. The intention is both to describe contemporary concerns in the terms of parishioners themselves and to critique them taking due account of the perspective of Anglican theology.

The Church in the parish

In respect of the first topic, the parishes were initially asked to read two passages from the Bible, Acts 2: 42 and 4: 22, emphasizing fellowship/common life, the Eucharist, prayer and healing. They were then asked to consider the nature of the Church and how far their own parish measured up to New Testament standards.

Among the key ideas evident in the responses, the most frequently mentioned mark of the Church was taken to be *'fellowship'*, cited by thirty-four parishes (47 per cent). Linking in with this, the central relation was felt to be that between *the Church and the outside world*, a focal concern expressed by thirty parishes (42 per cent). Since nothing in the discussion outline suggested mission or evangelism, this may imply that the contemporary

Church is less inward looking than is sometimes claimed. The third most prominent idea (from seventeen parishes) echoed the deanery reports (Chapter 5) in specifying the need for the Church to become *a teaching Church*. An 'outward' orientation was again manifested in the frequent mention of the notion of *community leadership and service*.

A further prominent idea was that of *healing*. It might be thought that this was prompted by the reading of passages from *Acts*, but this does not appear to be so. These were references to a healing ministry already practised by the parishes concerned, and it was notable that these mentions were often coupled with references to *preaching/witness* and *service*. Indeed, expressed in various ways there was a relatively widespread emphasis (also evident in deanery reports; see Chapter 5) on *faithful witness* as something that characterizes all parishes.

A rather different underlying theme concerned the absence in the Church of the supposed virtues of *the charismatic movement* (whatever its vices), especially the absence of the power of the Holy Spirit and of worship as the expression of joy. Some of the reports were determined to reject the approach of the charismatic and similar movements as being un-Anglican, but the very need to do so indicates that these parishes felt challenged by it. One parish recorded that its discussions began with 'an angry attack against enforced jollity and mateyness in church'. Another parish felt that it could hardly be expected to be boiling over with freshness and expectancy of a new 'movement', and went on: 'there is fear of the idea of revival because many Anglicans have heard of the emotionalism of [the Welsh revival of] 1904–5. How can you have a converted Anglican congregation with a lot of un-Anglican behaviour?' Put more positively, there is a desire in some quarters for worship to become an experience of joy without degenerating into what today would be called mass hysteria and what the eighteenth century called (pejoratively) 'enthusiasm'. How, indeed, can the local Church community be an expression of Christian love without degenerating into an 'enforced mateyness' which is intolerant of personal privacy and individual differences? How, in the words of one parish, can present-day churches 'be fired with the same enthusiasm in fellowship and witness [as the early Church] – ordinary people who were fired by the Holy Spirit with an enthusiasm which was infectious?'

By contrast with this focus, there was a (more 'Anglican'!) concern with *doctrine*. This was sometimes specifically mentioned, but it also underlay the widespread concern with teaching. One parish wrote:

> The Thirty Nine Articles [of Religion, which date from Elizabeth I and are set forth in the Book of Common Prayer (1662), to whose doctrine Welsh clergy are still required to assent] have lost their relevance, but there is a need for something to be put in their place, showing how we uphold the catholic creeds but are a reformed church. Clear statements on 'who is Jesus?' and 'why did he die?' would be helpful. We find such statements as 'saved by the blood of the Lamb' and 'being saved' quite meaningless.

Sincere believers were thus sometimes disoriented, unable to grasp present-day realities via the theological categories of some existing traditions. Beside the need, as they saw it, to experience the love of God and the fellowship of the faithful, was the need to understand, through their religion, the world in which they live and the problems that they face.

The nature of the Church
Issues raised for the Church in the modern era evidently include the expressive significance of worship, and the meaning and interpretation of doctrine. The charismatic movement presents a challenge to Anglican congregations and leads them to ask basic questions: in what ways can the Church change to permit what is felt to be an authentically Anglican expression of the power of the Holy Spirit?

The laity were anxious about the absence of the Spirit in worship. Their responses also show an absence of the Spirit from their understanding of the nature of the Church, which was remarkable for the lack of any sense of the Church as the Body of Christ. This doctrine involves the idea that it is through the gift of the Holy Spirit to His followers that they constitute the material bodily means whereby Christ continues to be present in the human world. If the gift of the Spirit is ignored, then the Church comes to be experienced as an association of individual followers of an absent God, rather than one who is alive and active within the Christian fellowship and whose action in the world is dependent on His followers. The relevant quotation from St Augustine was, however, supplied by one parish: 'Without God we cannot. Without us God will not.'

Clergy vocations

The introduction to the second topic drew attention to the 49 per cent decline in clergy numbers in Wales over thirty years and then asked the laity three questions, the first being whether they thought their parish was in any way responsible for this state of affairs.

The commonest response – given by 61 per cent of parishes – was one of indignation that they should be held responsible, followed by claims about how many candidates for the ministry their parish had produced. The second most frequent reaction was to accept that the parish was implicated, but as part of a vicious circle in which they were trapped. Institutional factors (low stipends in the past, poor working conditions, an over-emphasis on high academic ability) and 'social' factors (secularization, depopulation, the attractiveness of alternative occupations) had produced a fall in clergy numbers. This was accommodated by the grouping of parishes, but this in turn constituted a deterioration in working conditions that made the 'job' less attractive. Thus it emerges that, although parishes did not (in the main) feel responsible for the decline, they did feel, in many cases strongly, a responsibility to produce candidates for the ministry and were deeply concerned when they were unable to do so. However, only a small number of parishes affirmed that the ministry had to be financially supported, that training and maintaining candidates cost money and that parishes had a responsibility here also. A striking indication of lack of financial awareness was that only one parish showed any clear under-standing of the way in which clergy stipends are financed and of the role of parochial giving through the diocesan quota.

The laity were next asked how their parish could actively encourage vocations to the ordained ministry. Interestingly, behind many responses lay an ideal model of the candidate-producing parish, which would have:

a strong and deep prayer life;
well-attended and attractive worship;

thriving youth organizations;

an ordained ministry which was visible;

an incumbent who was enjoying himself and fulfilled by his ministry and who enjoyed good working conditions;

an incumbent who 'brought on' young people, and actively involved them in assisting with his activities as an incumbent (hence increasing 'visibility');

a congregation which had a strong concept of Christian vocation in the widest sense, so that all members were expected to have or to be seeking their specific Christian vocation;

a strong tradition of Bible study and of teaching the faith – what Christians believe and why they believe it;

young assistant clergy.

None of the parishes put forward so elaborate a model, but every element of it is to be found in the reports, which then proceeded either to claim that they were successful in producing candidates because some of these elements were present or to bemoan their absence. Many parishes did both, and produced a balanced picture of their strengths and weaknesses.

The third question on this topic asked whether people felt that the work pattern of the clergy should be changed. In response nearly a quarter of parishes said they could not answer because they did not know what that pattern was, but among the others there was considerable agreement that lay participation was needed to relieve clergy of duties not essential to their calling: 'A good priest is not necessarily a good accountant or estate manager.' Although widely recognized in principle, it was not always put into practice: for instance, by a small elderly congregation. Also, the most able lay people were often already under pressure from the demands of their secular work. These parishes suggested that clergy ought to have paid lay assistance. While a part-time secretary is probably appropriate for parochially based assistance, few could afford it; however, they could contribute to the cost of central facilities on which they could draw. Yet no one suggested that these be provided at the deanery level. There was a general assumption that to increase the role of the deanery was the first step on a slippery slope towards the abolition of the parochial system, and little recognition that a deanery centre could be a way of enhancing and preserving parochial ministry.

Team ministries were favoured by six parishes, but not as an answer to the problem of grouped benefices. Only one of these was in a rural diocese; the remainder were in the urban south. The advantages were seen as reduced clergy isolation and allowing the development of special gifts through permitting a degree of specialization. Finally, several parishes (perhaps reflecting the opinions of their incumbents; see Chapter 5) felt that clergy spent too much time on extra-parochial activities instead of being allowed to get on with their 'real job', which was seen as bounded by the parish. It seems never to have occurred to anyone that a life isolated from colleagues and confined to the limits of the local community could itself be a disincentive to would-be candidates for the ministry in a world of global communication and high-speed travel where all the really important events are seen, rightly or wrongly, to take place outside the locality.

A Christian vocation
In connection with clergy vocations, the main issue is recognized to be how to get out of the vicious circle of falls in clergy numbers, the grouping of parishes, reduced congregations, and a smaller pool of candidates for the ministry. However, the laity demonstrates a relative lack of awareness of how clergy stipends are financed and of the role of parochial giving through the quota. Although there are major difficulties in realizing the widely shared model of the 'candidate-producing' parish in practice, it does at least suggest a set of courses of action of which some will be possible in most parish situations.

In respect of clergy work patterns, the most popular response was that lay participation was needed to relieve clergy of duties not essential to their calling. However, there was little emphasis on the important idea of Christian vocation in a general sense, nor were clergy open about their vocations and the difficulties and agonies involved in their fulfilment. From a Christian point of view, vocations are not to be thought of as exclusive things characterized by 'job demarcation', as in the secular world. Sharing between clergy and laity is not to be confused with the incumbent sloughing off particular jobs to lay people to free himself for his pastoral and spiritual tasks which are of the essence of his calling. The point is that what is of the essence and cannot be sloughed off can to a degree be shared. For example, no one would suggest that the incumbent should not visit his flock but leave it to the laity, but it *is* an activity in which the laity can share.

It emerges that, by and large, the active Anglican laity do not think of the Church as simply a gathering of individuals who have made a personal commitment to Christ. Rather, that commitment is seen as coming about through participation in the life of the Church. On the other hand, the parishes tended to see the Church as a gathering of individual local churches, rather than the parish, as being a particular, local expression of the Church Universal. The associated tendency towards parochialism of local churches, the confinement of the concept of fellowship to the local congregation, at the expense of the fellowship between different parishes and dioceses, may constitute a disincentive to ordinands. The widespread parish view appears to be that clergy should not waste their time on deanery and diocesan matters: their place is with 'us here' not with 'them out there'. Of course, vocations are exercised through 'the daily round, the common task', but what of the idea that those activities need continually to be put in a wider context: that 'time out' is needed for clergy to enjoy the fellowship of others that comes from the sharing of experience and the interchange of ideas? The lay parish view arguably fails to confront the issue of finding means of bringing parochial clergy together in a way which supports them in their parochial ministry and enriches their lives.

Evangelism

On this topic lay members were asked, first, how the parish figure for Easter communicants (ECs) as a proportion of total population compared with an estimated all-Wales figure of 6.3 per cent; and, secondly, how that proportion would change if all baptized and confirmed members living locally were included. They were then asked to give their views on what should be done to return nominal members to the fold, and to bring in those from outside the Church.

On the first point, twenty-six out of seventy-two thought that, in their parish, the proportion formed of all residents by ECs was similar to the provincial average. Twenty thought their proportion was higher, and seventeen thought it lower, while nine did not know. Excluding 'don't knows', only seven out of thirty-six parishes in the more rural dioceses (19 per cent) thought their proportion lower, but in the more urban dioceses as many as twelve out of thirty-six (33 per cent) reckoned that their ECs formed a smaller proportion of their population than the provincial average. On this evidence the populations of the more urban dioceses may be seen to be more secularized than those of the more rural.

On the second point, twenty-eight parishes were unable to quantify the change that would occur if all baptized and confirmed residents regularly took Easter Communion. However, of the remaining forty-four, only thirteen thought that this inclusion would have a small effect, while thirty-one thought that if they could bring in all the baptized and confirmed persons in the community it would have a major effect, increasing the proportion of active Anglicans by between 10 and 60 per cent. In parishes in urban dioceses it was generally thought that bringing in non-attending members would make a substantial difference, but among those in rural dioceses less than half thought so, reinforcing the earlier conclusion that secularization was less advanced in rural areas.

Turning next to what could be done to return the lapsed to active membership, the most frequently mentioned courses of action were making personal approaches (23 per cent) and improving the 'attractiveness' of worship (30 per cent). In respect of the latter, what emerged particularly strongly was a recognition of a generational divide in preferred style of worship. This tended to be put in the language of 'young and old'. In the past the young have become old – that is, they have come to prefer the same style of worship as older worshippers when they themselves become old – but there is reason to believe that this will not happen to the same extent in future. Since about 1968 the young have become used to attending public performances of music which are far removed from those of their secular predecessors, let alone from contemporary church worship. These performances are designed to create ecstatic states in which participants have 'out of self' experiences and feel a loss of individuality, an occurrence which is more frequent the more 'charismatic' the performer(s). To many under the age of fifty-five, community singing, let alone choral evensong, is an alien experience, as alien as is contemporary popular music to many *over* fifty-five. Some of the laity argued the need for different age-related types of service, that for young people being somewhat less distant from the experiences of the rock generation and its successors than conventional Anglican worship. However, the need for family services was also frequently stressed, and with it the provision of facilities to encourage attendance, especially crèches, and transport for the elderly.

Only seven parishes mentioned perhaps the most obvious approach, which is to follow up baptisms and confirmations. One parish had tried this and been unsuccessful, but the rest thought it a way forward, viewing the occasional offices as evangelistic opportunities. What came across clearly was the failure of the Church, outside the offices themselves, to make baptized persons (or their parents) and confirmands feel that they were members of (in secular terms) an organization which valued and needed their participation. In most associations joining involves being kept in touch and urged to participate. If the active laity fail to behave in this way, it will reinforce the tendency for baptism and confirmation (for instance) to become for many mere empty rituals.

The responses in respect of what to do about the lapsed and about those having no religious conviction tended to overlap and were concerned with 'bringing people in' on the one hand, and turning people (who were already 'in') 'outward' on the other.

The general aim of responses in the first category was making parish life more attractive. This included emphasis on the strength and vigour of the spiritual life of the parish, Christianity as a religion of joy and love rather than moral condemnation, more visiting by both clergy and lay people, more lay participation in the sense of asking people to do things in and for the Church to show that they were valued, and the revival of Church-associated peripheral activities which people join for the activity but through which they come into contact with practising Christians. Two parishes recommended threatening closure of the church unless it was better supported! One parish reported the case of a parishioner who, when closure was threatened, handed over £10 with the words 'Peidiwch â chau'r eglwys nes i fi gael fy nghladdu'. ('Don't close the church till I'm dead and buried.')

The other broad category of responses was concerned with an 'outside orientation'. Better advertising, leaflet drops, better communication, better publicity, correcting negative images of Christianity and the Church caused by the media, were all mentioned here. However, so was the old-fashioned parish 'mission' and the newfangled 'community service' or 'community care' approaches. These parishes were not, it should be emphasized, putting the second of the two 'great commandments' (love thy neighbour) above the first (love God) or ignoring it altogether; nor were they advocating that the Church duplicate the functions of the social services. Indeed, one parish warned against the Church trying to do too much and doing badly what others could do better. However, the stress here was on the duty of the Church to show forth in its life Christ's love and compassion for all humanity. There were some situations which provided the Church with opportunities which it alone could take; but, more generally, such care and concern could best be shown, said several parishes, by working with others outside the Anglican Church – either ecumenically or with secular groups, or both.

Two other types of response also deserve mention. The first emphasized the need for the Church to come off the defensive and challenge secular society. The Church, it was felt, failed to present itself as a body of people with a faith and a vision which differentiated it from non-Christians. This was connected with the second response, which asked for much stronger leadership from dignitaries. However, although there was general recognition of the necessity of parishioners gearing themselves as much for 'mission as maintenance', the response to the challenge presented by secular society occasionally showed bafflement and despair. 'We are very sorry for the 86 per cent who have not heard of the Gospel, but we really don't see what we can do about it', said one parish with commendable frankness.

The Church and the world

Behind many replies, and explicit in others, was the need to 'break down the barrier between the Church and the community': that is (theologically), between the 'church' and 'world'. The point here is that Christians are required to be *in* the world but not *of* it. This gives rise to two dangers in Christian witness. In their anxiety not to be *of* the world they withdraw from it; but if they are not *in* it, they have not responded to the command 'Go ye into all the world and preach the Gospel.' The other danger is that in their concern to witness *in* the world they become *of* it. But if they are *of* the world, then they have nothing distinctive to say to the world; they fail to challenge the world. To these considerations must be added another one. The reason that many parishes were not *in* the world was not because they were sectarian, world-rejecting 'holy huddles' but because their members were drawn from a narrow range of social groups.

Throughout the answers on this topic ran the theme of the need for congregations to be more 'welcoming'. However, one does not get the impression that these congregations are not open and welcoming. In some cases, at least, it may be that what was being implied was the need to be more welcoming to people who do not come from the social groups that supply most of the existing Church members. In other words, there is awareness that congregations are often socially limited and need to have the membership broadened before they can witness to the faith effectively. It may be that the way forward is by widening the social composition of congregations through recruiting members from inactive baptized and confirmed first, and only then confronting the more difficult issue of preaching the Gospel to those with no contact with the Church. Until that has happened parishes may not be able to see how they can witness effectively to the unchurched.

Ways of increasing lay participation

The lay members were next presented with survey data showing the distribution of 'lay workers' in the Church in Wales (averaging 18.4 per benefice) and asked, in the light of these findings, how the members in their own parish could take a fuller part in the work and ministry of the Church. In response, 44 per cent said that their parish position was broadly satisfactory, many going on to detail those performing specific duties, including Sunday School teachers, persons administering Holy Communion, readers, association leaders, and PCC officers. They then said that there were certain problems, or scope for improvement, in some areas, chief of which was the concentration of lay participation among a core of lay people. These parishes were evidently relatively successful. The fact that such a large proportion of parishes was characterized by strong lay support suggests that in selecting parishes to take part in the study, rural deans had chosen 'strong' parishes as being more likely to return a full report, and it follows that the responding parishes, although geographically representative of the Province, may not present a true picture of the state of the Church, with regard to lay participation.

Among those making a suggestion as to the form that greater lay participation might take, one response predominated. Assisting clergy with parish visiting was mentioned by forty-two per cent. However, difficulties in this connection were noted: the need for lay training; the desire of the visited to be visited by the vicar; the unease of potential visitors at the usurpation of a traditional clergy role.

A further important idea expressed by four parishes was the need to uncover gifts possessed by the laity which they could be helped to use. This relates to the wider theme of Christian vocation. How is the individual to know what his or her vocation is? Laity need to be helped to discover these qualities and to know how they might be developed and employed, which is an essential part of helping them to discover their vocation. One parish objected to the use of the term 'lay ministry' (although it was not used in the discussion outline) on the grounds that 'ministry' was too 'high' a word to apply to lay activities. It may reasonably be wondered what they would have said about 'lay vocations'! Clearly the words ministry (service) and vocation (calling) are associated in the minds of some congregations uniquely with the clergy.

A point made by some parishes was that the contribution of the laity was taken for granted and people were not thanked. These remarks again fit in with the idea of the laity as 'the vicar's helpers'. If the laity are the Church, however, whose minister the vicar is, they should be thanking him – not vice versa. Yet, at another level there is, of course, a valid and important point here. The Christian community in that place should, through its representative (the vicar), show an appreciation of the services given by its members, and ensure that their contribution is properly acknowledged.

Clergy and laity

It emerges from the reports that the laity continue to think of themselves as second-class citizens within the Church, as servants primarily of the vicar – not any more, perhaps, in the sense of being the vicar's social inferiors, but in the sense that the most they can do is to assist the vicar in doing his or her job, which is to be the Church. It is not being claimed that this describes a doctrine which people hold, but it is being suggested that people act as if this is what they believe.

It seems there is some way to go in getting the roles of clergy and laity as defined within Anglican theology properly understood by lay members. The laity rightly perceive the clergy to have a sacred (set-apart) calling and unique role. But they tend to see that role as being the Church for the laity. There is a failure to recognize that the distinctive task of clergy is to represent the local church to itself and to the wider church, and the wider church to the local church, and that it is from this representative function that the unique liturgical and doctrinal roles of the clergy derive.

Worship

The discussion outline stated that worship was at the heart of the life of the Church and then asked parishes to evaluate their own worship and consider it in relation to non-churchgoers.

Approximately 85 per cent of parishes seemed on the whole satisfied, while 15 per cent were classified as being 'uneasy' about the existing form and pattern. A striking aspect was the near-absence of complaints about the liturgy, which, by contrast, were forthcoming from clergy in some deanery reports. However, there was no complacency about their existing patterns of service provision. On the contrary, the reports were testimony to the amount of care and thought that had produced the existing pattern. Reports typically described this in detail, relating it to the needs and preferences of different social groups in the benefice (Welsh/English; young/old; traditionalist/modern; locals/incomers), giving arguments for and against different types of arrangements and their experience of them, and concluding that it was about right at the moment; but they sometimes went on to make proposals for improvement. What comes through strongly, both from the broadly satisfied and from those classified as being 'uneasy' with the existing pattern, is the need for variety in liturgical provision. 'Variety' sometimes referred to the variety of weekly services, sometimes to variation over a monthly cycle, and sometimes to the need for many more 'special' services during the year.

The main tension, evident within and between reports, concerned the need to make a service more 'lively', more 'informal', 'warmer', more joyful – in a word, more 'attractive', and the need to offer to God what was felt to be the best in worship: for services to be beautiful, dignified, profound. This was not a crude opposition, but there was a sober recognition of the fact that liturgical practices and forms highly beneficial to deepening the spirituality of the instructed faithful were sometimes positively unhelpful to those on the fringe of religious life, and that the needs of the latter were just as important as the needs of the former. The requirement to provide for both these groups was the most important underlying reason for the demand for 'variety'. However, the variety included, in many parishes, 'family services' and most expressed the need for a standard form for such services which could provide a coherent liturgical framework on which parishes could elaborate.

Parishes divided 55 per cent affirmative and 45 per cent negative in response to whether they would be happy to invite a non-Church neighbour to their regular Sunday worship, but affirmative answers were frequently qualified by mentions of ways in which services could be made more accessible to outsiders. Just under one-third favoured the introduction of non-traditional practices into traditional worship, or felt that freedom to experiment should be permitted to them. However, there was wide recognition of the problems involved in innovation. It would be easy to get a majority in some parishes in favour of the view that the traditional liturgy was old fashioned and out of date, but there would be no majority for its replacement by any other form of worship, since those voting for change wanted change in different directions, and any specific change would alienate more than it pleased. One parish reported that it had introduced, successfully, special youth services but noted wryly that these were not attended by those who had requested their introduction. Young people were, one parish remarked, notably fickle; fashions changed with bewildering rapidity. However, there was, above and beyond this, a recognition of the value of a traditional liturgy even among those who were keenly aware of and worried by its limitations. One parish referred to 'babies and bathwater', of the danger of losing what was valuable in traditional forms in an attempt to rid them of their alleged 'off-putting' character in respect of non-believers.

Forms of worship

In respect of the views expressed on worship, agreement might be reached on the following points. As a form of Christian life and witness Anglicanism has been shaped by its mode of worship, which links the Churches of the Anglican Communion with each other and with both the Catholic and the Protestant past; it cannot lightly be abandoned. By its nature it is directed to God, not man. It is, however, the duty of the Church to share the knowledge and love of God and to show it forth in worship, and this it fails to do if it narrowly confines itself to traditional forms. It follows that alongside the latter there should exist forms of worship which can include 'outsiders' and constitute a bridge between the Church and the 'world'. This requires that over the liturgical year a variety of forms of worship should be provided of which some are deliberately inclusive rather than exclusive. Suggestions made by parishes included special services associated with the great Christian festivals, and special 'guest services'. All services should have, though, a proper liturgical form and shape. There is, therefore, a need for (a) alternatives to the existing offices and Eucharistic liturgy which should differ only in that they provide a greater scope for variation according to occasion and circumstance; and (b) properly worked-out frameworks for 'special' services which can be used creatively by parishes. Such looser liturgical forms make it possible for those who use them to supply elements which provide contemporary relevance so that the 'substance' remains unchanging but the 'accidents' are always in tune with the contemporary world. However, it is not the job of Christians to make services attractive in the worldly sense.

Too many buildings

Some information on the numbers of churches, parsonages and other buildings possessed by the Church in Wales as a whole was presented to the lay members and they were then asked, 'Do the buildings you have meet the needs of the parish?'

In evaluating the responses, it is again necessary to point out that rural deans chose 'stronger' parishes to take part in the study and this does have a bearing on attitudes and circumstances concerning buildings. Parishes felt to be 'weak' are frequently those subsequently grouped, creating not one strong benefice but a group of weak parishes. These are precisely the benefices where buildings exceed the needs of the congregation but are difficult to close because of the dispersed nature of the latter. These parishes are not well represented in the study. It is, therefore, not surprising that thirty-four out of seventy-two of the stronger parishes from which information was elicited considered that their buildings were 'about right' for their needs. Three of the remaining thirty-eight said they needed more churches, and nearly a quarter, even of this arguably biased sample, said they needed fewer.

A key theme over and above sheer numbers was the problem posed by churches being in the wrong place, and this was true not merely of urban areas where the centre of gravity had shifted over the last two hundred years, leaving a large, ancient church on the edge of a modern settlement, but also in rural areas where population shifts had left the largest place of worship at one end of the present benefice – and in some cases the most suitable hall at the other. One parish wanted to knock all its buildings down and build a new church and hall in the middle of the area; but, cost considerations aside, they knew that the congregations of each church would never stand for it.

The most significant finding is, however, that nearly half of those with felt problems were dissatisfied because they had no adequate hall. Similarly, the question of provision for activities other than worship was mentioned as important by the majority of those who were satisfied. These parishes either had a hall or halls in the right place, were conveniently located near a village hall, community centre or school which they used, or had adapted part of a large church, or built rooms on to a smaller church which served their purpose. Those complaining of the lack of a hall had been unable to solve their problems in these ways, either because of the location of the church or the unsuitability of its buildings, or both. What comes across particularly clearly therefore is the necessity for 'non-worship' buildings for both fellowship and mission, and the severe difficulties which both more and less 'successful' parishes experience because of the lack of these facilities.

An administrative burden

Despite the severe problems relating to the number and position of church buildings, the parochial reports did not complain, as clergy had done, about the financial and administrative burden of maintaining buildings. There are two clear reasons for this. These matters loom large in the minds of some clergy, not because they are necessarily all that time-consuming but because clergy feel they are not their real 'job' at all. Again, parishes are relatively sanguine about these matters because some of them are quite content to let clergy shoulder a burden which arguably should be that of the laity. Nevertheless, one can infer from the reports that the laity are thoroughly involved in the policy decisions about buildings if not in their day-to-day administration; to which the clergy would doubtless respond that it is precisely the administration rather than the policy that is such a burden.

Money

The discussion outline drew attention to the fact that personal giving in the Church amounted (in 1988) to an average of £2.69 per week, which met 50 per cent of the overall expenditure. It affirmed that giving is a part of Christian service and then asked: 'How can Church giving become a higher priority in personal budgeting in your parish?'

Many of the responses were of a familiar kind: 'People give as much as they feel they can and nothing more can be expected'; 'Giving is very good in this parish since it is approximately £2 per week per person'; 'The group was greatly surprised at the statistics since our giving is approximately 80p per week per head and we are able to meet all our commitments.' Reports also said that 'giving is a personal matter', a 'delicate subject', 'you can't tell people how much to give', often as reasons for simply issuing vague exhortations.

The reports taken together show, on the contrary, the absolute necessity of there being clear guidelines to provide a background against which individuals can make responsible choices. If Church people in Wales give on average a specified sum per week and I do not, I have to ask myself whether I should. There may, of course, be reasons for a negative answer: I have only a pension; I am a single parent raising two children; I am unemployed. Six parishes mentioned these factors as affecting their level of giving. Equally, the question may arise: 'Should I not give more? Why? Because I earn substantially more than the average income.' Two parishes affirmed the necessity of getting the better-off to give more than the average. But should personal giving be evaluated in this way? Is not the average too low? Comparison should be made, some parishes said, with take-home pay, or pay after basic necessary expenditure had been deducted, or with the amount spent on luxuries.

Twenty parishes highlighted the necessity for information and teaching on the issue of giving. However, it was noticeable that the emphasis was on information about ecclesiastical finances: people have got to realize how much everything costs and be told where the money goes. This may be contrasted with the central Christian idea that all they have comes from God and that they have a duty to give a proportion of what they have back to God to support His work in the world. Only nine parishes were operating or committed to operating stewardship programmes having this teaching as their central principle. Only fourteen parishes mentioned covenanting as the way forward, and one parish said that it was not properly understood.

A number of other important points arose. First, there was a conflict between giving to the Church and giving to other charitable causes. Should people give to the Church, and the Church support charities, and, if not, what proportion of an individual's planned giving should go to the Church? Secondly, five parishes said the problem was lack of people rather than the absence of generosity, while others pointed to the presence of two categories of Church members: the small core who committed time, talents and money, and peripherals who came along for a free ride. Increased financial giving was associated, other parishes pointed out, with increased lay participation; other involvements resulted in financial commitment. Two parishes asked whether those who used Church facilities only for the occasional offices should be asked to contribute to their upkeep.

Thirdly, one parish pointed to an interesting dilemma. If you say to people, 'we have to pay for the service which is provided', they resent paying the quota. If you get the message across that the central authority pays a large proportion of the cost of the clergy and the bulk of a quota is a contribution to that cost, then this destroys their sense of responsibility for their local church. On a fourth, allied point, several parishes stated that 'things are different in the country'. 'Special efforts' to raise funds for various purposes are essential elements of village social life, and this makes it difficult to emphasize the importance of planned individual giving unrelated to a specific need. Other parishes echoed this theme, praising the responses of their people to crises like burst boilers and leaky roofs, but confessing to having made no progress at all on the regular personal-giving front.

Stewardship

The call to stewardship is not merely jargon for 'planned giving'. It involves the notion that Christians are called to the stewardship of God's gifts. Stewardship in the full sense is still an idea foreign to most parishes. But its practical implication in either its restricted or its full sense requires guidelines if personal, private decisions are to be taken responsibly. In this connection it is recognized that information about ecclesiastical finances, and teaching on the issue of giving, are needed.

Conclusion

This chapter has considered a number of characteristics of the Church in Wales at the parochial level, as evidenced by the views of its most active members – those elected to PCCs. In spite of the fact that the sample is probably skewed towards the more successful and lively parishes, the picture that emerges is none the less, from the Church's point of view, an optimistic one. The PCCs emerge as lively, concerned and willing to innovate. However, the data reveal two major and related problems.

The parishes are clearly aware that they live in a changing

world. Established institutions, whether commercial or political, currently stress the need for 'modernization' ('new Labour, new Britain') as a response to these changes. However, institutions which are essentially conservative – stressing, that is, the preservation of past beliefs and values – whether they are world religions (or branches thereof) or political parties (such as the British Conservative Party in the 1970s and the late 1990s), face a dilemma, between the horns of which they must seek to escape. To refuse to change will safeguard their traditional beliefs and values at the price of increasing their perceived irrelevance, which in turn will result in declining numbers, falling revenues and eventual extinction. However, to 'modernize' – that is, to abandon that which it is their mission to conserve – will leave them without a distinctive message and lose them the allegiance of their traditional supporters. Small wonder, then, that some of the parishes described themselves as 'baffled'. This dilemma the 'grass roots' share with Church leaders as those leaders attempt to adapt traditional morality to changed circumstances.

The second problem that the data reveal is that the laity lack a solid grasp of the nature of the Church as a divine institution. This creates difficulties in their attempt to resolve the first problem. If a church is to 'modernize' without compromising that which it exists to preserve, its members need to distinguish in the tradition they have received those elements that are essential to their faith from other elements that owe their existence to past circumstances. This they cannot do unless they have the sort of grasp of the essentials of their faith that will enable them to distinguish one from the other.

It may be thought odd to draw this conclusion from data which tell us about the problems perceived by the laity in the practice of their faith but (by contrast to some of the data of Chapter 7) do not deal primarily with their understanding of its doctrine. It only appears odd, however, if one ignores the nature of the Church as a divine institution: that is to say, if one fails to recognize that a Church is an institution whose social order is regarded by its members not as a human means to divine ends but as being itself sacred and God-given.

The nature of the right relationship between the roles of clergy and of laity is, therefore, simultaneously a doctrinal and an intensely practical matter. Its importance can hardly be overestimated in a Church whose social circumstances demand that it be evangelistically active, and whose economic circumstances require that it respond to that demand with far lower clergy-to-laity and clergy-to-population ratios than have previously existed.

The twentieth century has seen what amounts to the renegotiation of the roles of ministers and members in all denominations. It may be argued that it was precisely because of this renegotiation that some commentators have seen the ministry to have been 'in crisis'. In the previous chapter we have argued that the clergy are not in crisis and that this is connected to the fact that the Church faced a crisis at the beginning of the nineties with which it has continued to grapple throughout the decade. This chapter demonstrates that the laity are not in crisis either. This is not surprising, since the roles of clergy and laity are defined in terms of each other. It may be said that the Church in Wales faced a crisis at the beginning of the nineties not because of the renegotiation of the relationship between the roles of clergy and laity but because that renegotiation had not gone far enough.

There can be little doubt that the Church is on the whole well served by its clergy, and little doubt too in most parishes of the commitment and devotion of the laity. Unfortunately, the most common understanding of that relationship is that it is the duty of the laity to support the clergy in their sacred ministry of being the Church on the laity's behalf. Until that understanding of the relationship central to the life of the Church is reversed, there is little hope that the gifts of all the members of the Anglican *laos*, whether clerical or lay, can be mobilized for the tasks of either 'maintenance' or 'mission'.

7

The characteristics, attitudes and social values of the laity

The approach adopted in Chapter 6 to the understanding of lay attitudes involves examining reports from PCCs of discussions of a set of issues concerning the life of the contemporary Church. Insights were provided into issues and problems facing the Church in a modern, predominantly secular society, and the contribution that the active laity were making, and might make, to their solution. In this chapter a complementary approach is adopted, as we present survey evidence of the social characteristics and attitudes, both religious and secular, of the active laity. Attention is given to both objective characteristics (such as sex, age, ability to speak Welsh) and subjective ones (such as opinions about aspects of Church life, or the power of trade unions). Of course, the subjective and objective connect up because expressed attitudes are partly to be understood by an appreciation of individuals' social origins and biographies. However, importantly, both the social characteristics and the religious attitudes of the laity have a bearing on their ability to contribute to the Church's evangelistic mission, which it is a primary purpose of this chapter to assess. With this in mind it is germane, for instance, to inquire whether the active laity have a sex/age profile which is such as to promote the dissemination of their views to up-and-coming generations, and also whether their religious views could be said to accord with the Anglican theological tradition (and are thus broadly aligned with those of the clergy), while facilitating interpretations and innovations (for instance, in respect of ecumenism) which may be necessary in modern conditions. Hence there is a need for information of a social and demographic type, but also for greater insight into 'lay theology'.

A secondary purpose of this chapter is to increase understanding of the 'structure of thought' of the laity in a way which takes in not simply the religious but also the secular sphere. In this connection it is a familiar fact that religious communities share doctrine and that this may underlie judgements on ostensibly 'secular' matters. More specifically, doctrinal differences have been shown to give rise to some broad variations in social and political attitudes. Indeed, an early and influential theme of the sociology of religion consists of a broad contrast between the secular implications of major world religions, which differ in their tendency to enjoin involvement in the world or to be 'other-worldly' (Weber 1963, ch. xvi; Parsons 1951, 368–78; Bellah 1957 and 1970). Again, adherents of the various denominations and sects belonging to a broader religious tradition, and found within a single society, have been shown often to exhibit patterned differences in their outlook on social and political issues (Argyle 1958; Lenski 1961). As implied above, these last may originate partly from the differing social locations of the religious groups concerned, but doctrinal differences tend to be implicated as well. This is almost invariably the case, given the fundamental role of religion in legitimating behaviour in other institutional spheres. However, although the broader theme of a link between religious and secular ideas is a familiar one, what is altogether less well documented is how it expresses itself within the context of a single religious community. In other words, exactly how do variations in both religious and secular ideas within such a community connect up? This is the issue addressed in relation to the Church in Wales in the latter part of the chapter.

The data in this chapter are derived from a separate survey of 'the laity'. The population surveyed was not restricted to the 'active' laity – those who held some office or performed some function in the benefices included in the survey; nor was it so extensive as to include all adherents of the Church in Wales – that is, those who communicated (at least at Easter). It was directed rather at *practising* adherents: those who attend church faithfully Sunday by Sunday. These members of the regular congregation may be termed 'the faithful'.

THE SURVEY OF THE LAITY

In order to provide a representative sample, a random sample of thirty of the Church's 604 benefices was first drawn, in such a way as to ensure that all the six dioceses were equally represented. Participating benefices were then asked to distribute a copy of a questionnaire to each adult attending the principal service at each of the benefice's churches on Advent Sunday, 1991. A 50 per cent sample was later taken of the forms completed and returned by each benefice. Prior calculation had suggested that this procedure would yield information on a lay sample of approximately 1,000. In fact the number of questionnaires becoming available for analysis proved to be 803 (because, in the event, four of the chosen benefices failed to respond), but this was judged to be large and representative enough for statistical purposes.

The questionnaire included three main sections. The first of these was the longest and elicited information concerning the personal and social characteristics of the respondents; also included were questions about religious practice. There followed fifteen questions, distributed in random order, on religious attitudes, so designed as together to yield information on five topics: the nature of the Church; its structure; ecumenism (or Christian unity); change in the Church; and the relationship between Church and 'world'. Previous discussions had suggested that these were the strategically important issues underlying the identity and present life of the Church and, in particular, those central to the response of the laity to the call to evangelism. A further section contained questions on secular matters – social and political issues – elaborated on below.

Religious practice

It may reasonably be wondered whether the methods used did yield a sample of those who were indeed 'the faithful'. The answers to the questions about religious practice provide information which permits the resolution of this issue. Ninety-four per cent of respondents claimed to worship regularly; 82 per cent said they prayed regularly outside church services; 83 per cent claimed to set aside a part of their income for the Church or other charitable purposes; 72 per cent said they took an active part in

Church life; and 63 per cent claimed to participate in some form of community service. Bearing in mind that those attending a service will never on any occasion consist solely of 'the faithful', these are remarkably high figures and indicate that the method adopted did reach the target group. However, given that a sample of 'the faithful' had indeed been drawn, one further indicator of religious practice becomes more striking. Respondents were also asked whether they read the Bible regularly, and only 45 per cent replied in the affirmative. Therefore, if it was once the case that practising Christians were 'people of the Book', this would not appear to be true today of the Anglican faithful in Wales.

In respect of four out of six of these religious behaviour variables there was a statistically significant difference (at the 5 per cent level or higher) between the responses of the two sexes, in each case women being the more active religiously. Thus the figures for those worshipping regularly were 96 per cent for females and 92 per cent for males; for those praying regularly outside religious services the proportions were 86 per cent for females and 74 per cent for males. Also, more women than men set aside part of their income (86 per cent compared with 79 per cent) and participated in community service (66 per cent and 57 per cent respectively). Again, in five out of the six cases there was a statistically significant correlation with age, with older people being the more active religiously. For instance, the proportion worshipping regularly rose from 87 per cent for those under twenty-five to 98 per cent for those aged over seventy-four. The exceptional variable was participation in community service, but even in that case the proportion involved rose to age sixty-five but then declined, no doubt the downturn being due to more widespread infirmity among the aged. In one case a religious behaviour variable had a statistically significant association with marital status: it transpired that the proportion claiming to set aside part of their income was higher among the widowed (91 per cent) than others, and lower among the single (72 per cent) and divorced (75 per cent).

Secular characteristics

Many of the demographic and social characteristics of the laity were as expected. They were found to be disproportionately elderly and female (cf. Greeley 1992; Davie 1994, ch.7).

Altogether 37 per cent were aged sixty-five or over (compared with about one-fifth of the general population), while 40 per cent were aged between forty-five and sixty-four and 23 per cent between eighteen and forty-four. The sex ratio was almost exactly 1:2, with 34 per cent male and 66 per cent female. As regards marital status, the most striking feature was the tiny proportion of divorced and separated persons, only 3 per cent; 68 per cent were married, 12 per cent single, and, as one would expect in such an elderly sample, as many as 17 per cent were widowed persons. The main point to emerge from the exploration of the interrelationships between these variables was that men were better represented in the youngest age group (where there were 66 men to every 100 women) than in the older ones (46 men per 100 women). This pattern is probably explained by the greater mortality of men, combined with the fact that they more often attended church as a member of a married couple.

As well as being disproportionately elderly and female, this sample of the laity had in the main been remarkably stable geographically. A massive 62 per cent had been resident in their present parish for more than twenty years, and 33 per cent had been there for over forty years; only 19 per cent had been resident there for less than ten years. This cannot be accounted for simply on the grounds of age, but accords well with what is often asserted about Anglican and particularly Welsh Anglican, allegiance: that it is intimately bound up with a sense of place. This should not be overemphasized, however: 30 per cent of the sample had been born outside Wales, made up of 2 per cent who hailed from north-east England, and 4 per cent from Scotland, Ireland and outside the UK, the other 24 per cent being distributed fairly equally between the remaining four English regions. If anything, those from outside Wales constituted a slightly larger proportion in the more rural dioceses.

The predominantly 'Welsh' character of 'the faithful' becomes even clearer when the responses to questions on language and ethnicity are considered: 41 per cent of the sample claimed to be able to speak Welsh either fluently or partly. The question asked on this topic in the last census was differently worded, but there is nevertheless good reason to believe that these respondents are rather better versed in the Welsh language than the Welsh population as a whole, only 19 per cent of whom, according to the

1991 census, claimed to speak Welsh. Indeed, this was likely to be the case given that the incidence of Welsh speaking increases with age. In response to a further question it transpired that 66 per cent of respondents considered themselves to be Welsh, while 26 per cent felt that they were English, and 8 per cent indicated other ethnic identities.

A further set of secular characteristics on which the survey provided information consisted of employment status, occupation, income and education. In this connection the first distinguishing feature of the laity was only to be expected in view of their age: 47 per cent of them were retired. Only 38 per cent were in employment, 24 per cent full-time and 14 per cent part-time; also the proportion of unemployed was, at 3 per cent, below the national average. Similarly revealing was the fact that, of those reporting past or present employment, 79 per cent indicated non-manual occupations, and only 21 per cent manual ones. The inference that the sample was fairly heavily 'middle class' is also suggested by the high figures for those who had left full-time education at eighteen (13 per cent) or over that age (24 per cent). True, there was a certain balance in that not dissimilar proportions had left school at fifteen (16 per cent) or even younger (20 per cent), but this was only to be expected given the elderly character of these church attenders. The income figures too ranged widely, but because the sample contained many retired people it was not as privileged in terms of income as the occupation figures might suggest: 46 per cent had incomes (in 1991) of less than £10,000 per year, and 28 per cent of below £6,000; on the other hand, 22 per cent had incomes of £20,000 or more.

The information that was collected from respondents on age of baptism and confirmation provides clear evidence of the predominantly long-term nature of their Church involvement. All but 2 per cent of them had been baptized, including 79 per cent at under two years, and only 7 per cent as adults; again, all but 5 per cent had been confirmed, including only 3 per cent who were adults at the time. The past failure of the Church to penetrate the secular world is illustrated by the fact that only 1 per cent of respondents had non-Christian parents. On the other hand, fully 77 per cent were of Anglican parentage, while a further 14 per cent of parents belonged to Protestant Nonconformist denominations, 3 per cent were Roman Catholics, and 5 per cent belonged to other Christian denominations. (The last figure may seem rather high, but the Welsh religious scene has in the past been characterized by the strength of a number of small religious groups, such as Quakers, Unitarians, Christian Scientists, Seventh Day Adventists and Brethren to which, in recent times, have been added several charismatic groups and evangelical fellowships.)

The implications of these figures are clear. In terms of secular characteristics those under-represented among the laity included men, the young, the economically active, the working class and the unemployed. However, the respondents were by no means rich, partly because so many were retired. It is also clear that the laity does not consist of the expatriate English and that the Church in Wales is unquestionably a Welsh Church in terms of both identity and language, in spite of the effects of Welsh out-migration and English in-migration.

Nevertheless, the unrepresentativeness of the laity must impose severe limits on their capacity to contribute to the Church's evangelistic mission. Their geographical mobility is evidently low, and because so many are not economically active or are women, or both, their social lives are likely to be centred on the domestic sphere and the neighbourhood. Communication on the subject of religion is widely considered to be difficult even in favourable circumstances, and the problem can only be increased by generational barriers and differing class cultures.

The differences in the position of the sexes revealed by this study present a particular challenge to the Church, for a continuing failure to attract men arguably combines with a failure to accord women their rightful place. Among those sampled, women were more active in terms of religious practice and community service, but this greater commitment did not appear to be reflected in their involvement in the Church's organizational life, which was the same as that of men. This finding tends to support the claim which is sometimes made that, even over and above the composition of the ordained ministry (which now includes a minority of women), the Church tends to be male-dominated (Aldridge 1987). There is evidently a need to afford the members of the Church's majority sex (including, it must be stressed, the elderly and retired as well as young professionals) the opportunity to participate at all levels according to their real abilities rather than according to those traditionally ascribed to them.

Religious attitudes

The general approach in the study to assessing attitudes in the religious sphere was to explore what has already been correctly termed 'lay theology'. In this connection it was fully appreciated that few Christians are professional theologians; nor are they, in most cases, intellectuals in the sense of being interested in ideas for their own sake. However, it was judged that, in being 'the faithful', the respondents were interested in making sense of their lives and of the world around them in Christian terms. Also, the achievement of genuinely religious goals within and beyond the Church community must rest upon the communication of theological issues. Within the clear limitations of the survey method, an attempt was therefore made to tap this Christian sense which the members of the laity made of their lives.

As indicated above, fifteen questions were asked which together were intended to explore ideas on five key topics. Each question took the form of an attitude statement with which the respondents were invited to indicate agreement or disagreement on a five-point scale (see appendix to this chapter). Three statements were presented randomly on each topic (interspersed with other statements), usually taking the form of two 'polar' positions and an intermediate one. For instance, there were three statements designed to express respondents' conceptions as to the nature of the Church (Set A). The first, held to represent a 'catholic' position, referred to authority, tradition and the sacraments. The third, reckoned to present an 'evangelical' position, referred to the believer's personal relationship with Jesus. The second statement expressed the view that Anglicans needed to get the balance right between these two types of positions.

Table 7.1 summarizes responses to questions on the five topics, and it is appropriate at this point to consider each in turn. It must be stressed that respondents were not asked to choose between the three positions on each issue, but merely to agree or disagree with each one. Although at the questionnaire-design stage they were taken to be alternatives, it was, of course, for respondents to exercise their own judgements. In respect of the first topic, the pattern of responses was reasonably straightfor-ward: it is apparent that roughly one-third of respondents agreed with the catholic position, but a similar number disagreed with it; the same was true for the evangelical position. On the other hand, about two-thirds agreed with the position seen as intermediate and only a few disagreed. Hence the laity, in favouring the *via media*, appeared to be reassuringly Anglican. However, further analysis reveals that just under one-tenth of respondents approved both the 'evangelical' and the 'catholic' statements, suggesting that it would be over-simple to infer that traditional theological oppositions have a secure place within the conscious-ness of the contemporary laity.

Table 7.1   Lay responses to religious-attitude statements (per cent)

Topic			Position 1	Position 2	Position 3
A.	Church		'catholic'	mid	'evangelical'
		agree	36.3	69.5	37.8
		disagree	33.3	7.5	35.5
B.	Structure		body of Christ	collection of parishes	collection of individuals
		agree	92.0	30.7	64.7
		disagree	1.1	35.6	17.4
C.	Change		against	mid	for radical change
		agree	39.7	50.3	33.5
		disagree	37.0	16.0	37.8
D.	Ecumenism		against	mid	for
		agree	15.5	53.1	48.9
		disagree	67.3	28.0	28.1
E.	World		reject	evangelize	serve
		agree	41.4	90.4	96.6
		disagree	31.6	1.8	1.2

The responses on the 'structure' topic (Set B) were more complex, with an overwhelming majority endorsing the statement that the Church was 'the body of Christ'. In addition, a large majority agreed with one or other of the remaining two statements to the effect that the Church was either an aggregate of parish congregations or an aggregate of believing individuals. In fact, the respondents divided up roughly two to one in favour of the latter view. Hence, the 'congregational' approach was less often favoured than an individualist one. However, any suggestion of a bias towards individualism must be qualified, given that virtually all these respondents also affirmed the 'body of Christ' statement.

In relation to the topic of change in the Church, the pattern of responses (Set C) has some similarities with that concerning the nature of the Church. The more 'extreme' statements were again assented to by one-third or more of respondents, but a similar proportion dissented. The conservative position affirmed resistance to the idea of the Church keeping up with the times, while the position of radical change referred to the rejection of the past and its traditions. Almost exactly half agreed with the intermediate position: since the world is changing, the Church also must change; but as many as one-sixth of the respondents disagreed. On this evidence the issue of change is more divisive than are the traditional doctrinal issues.

Similarly divisive is the issue of ecumenism (Set D). Here, the statement in favour referred to divisions being a scandal, and the need for the creation of a single Christian Church, while that opposed to ecumenism implied that Christian divisions should be overcome by everyone becoming an Anglican. The intermediate position stressed a need for partnership, while allowing scepticism as to the effectiveness of institutional co-operation. The pattern of responses was reasonably clear-cut in that the position of outright opposition was largely rejected (by two-thirds), but each of the other positions was endorsed by about half, but rejected by more than a quarter. Hence, the major cleavage was between the 'ecumaniacs' (as their opponents call them) on the one hand, and those who, while favouring co-operation between denominations, consider attempts to extend institutional co-operation a waste of time.

The fifth topic concerned the relation between the church and the world (Set E). In this case the first statement said that it was the job of the Church to fight against the world outside the Church and was opposed by one which stressed the duty of the Church to serve everyone. A further statement saw the world as the target for evangelism. Clearly the respondents did not see the latter position, with its conception of the world as an audience for the Gospel, as incompatible with the notion of the world as an object for loving service, since over 90 per cent agreed with both. However, over two-fifths of respondents endorsed a statement concerned with the fallen nature of the world, and of these a large majority also agreed with one or both of the other two statements. This provides further evidence that historical theological divisions are far from the consciousness of many lay members.

In an attempt further to extend understanding of the mind of the laity, the response patterns on each topic were examined, and then consolidated into a single classification. When this was done some patterns were unclassifiable because of partial or complete non-response. Those who for this reason could not be classified averaged 23 per cent of respondents per topic. In addition, there were those who fully responded on a topic, but whose response patterns implied a rejection of the way of thinking which lay behind the set of questions posed. This was true for an average of 19 per cent on each issue. Nevertheless it proved possible to develop for each topic a refined classification of opinions based on the rationale of the set of questions, which did apply to a majority of respondents. The resultant distribution is shown in Table 7.2, together with the proportion of the total sample who could be so classified on each issue.

In respect of the nature of the Church, the largest category was unequivocally 'Anglican' in the *via media* sense, but it proved possible to distinguish between 'catholic' and 'Anglo-catholic' positions as well as between 'evangelical' and 'protestant' ones. On structure, the refined classification makes it clear that the largest proportion combined conventional Anglican theology with a tendency towards individualism. In relation to both change and ecumenism three substantial groups emerged with differing opinions. Although change is a divisive issue, this was the topic that seems to have generated least confusion in the minds of respondents, judging by the smaller proportion rejecting the thought structure of the set of statements. On ecumenism the proportion who emerged as unequivocally against was small. On the relation between church and world the predominant tendency was evidently to view the latter both as an audience for evangelism and as an object of service.

Table 7.2   Opinions on five topics, and proportion of sample so classified

A. Church	%	B. Structure	%	C. Change	%	D. Ecumenism	%	E. World	%
catholic	8.3	parochial	8.2	conservative	28.8	against	4.4	service	11.0
Anglo-catholic	14.8	parochial/ Anglican	7.0	conservative/ moderate	5.7	against/ moderate	3.9	service/ evangelism	83.6
Anglican	46.7	Anglican	30.7	moderate	28.8	moderate	29.9	evangelism	3.1
evangelical	22.6	Anglican/ individualist	50.9	moderate/ radical	31.8	moderate/ favourable	34.6	evangelism/ reject	2.3
protestant	7.6	individualist	3.1	radical	4.9	favourable	27.2	reject	0.0
TOTAL	100.0	TOTAL	99.9	TOTAL	100.0	TOTAL	100.0	TOTAL	100.0
Number	433	Number	483	Number	533	Number	431	Number	421
% of total sample	53.9	% of total sample	60.2	% of total sample	68.9	% of total sample	53.7	% of total sample	52.4

A further area of analysis concerned whether respondents' positions on these issues were related. It transpired that out of ten possible comparisons between responses to pairs of the five topics, only two were statistically significant ($p < 0.05$). The first such relationship was between the 'structure' and 'change' issues (Sets B and C). Those who simply saw Church structure as 'the body of Christ' were less often conservative and more often in favour of moderate change than those who saw the Church also as a collection of individuals, whether people or parishes. The second significant relationship was between responses to the 'Church' and ecumenism issues (Sets A and D). Of those classified as 'catholic' a lower proportion was in favour of ecumenism than of those judged 'Anglican'; an above-average proportion of those classified as 'protestant' was also against ecumenical initiatives.

The latter relation conforms to common experience: the more theologically conservative among those of either of the two main traditions are less often in favour of the unity movement. For the catholic tradition, other views tend to be 'errors'; while for protestants, visible and institutional unity tends to be viewed as unimportant, given an emphasis on the individual rather than on the group. The relation between individualism and dislike of change is perhaps less readily interpretable. However, what seems to emerge is that those prepared to view structure in purely aggregate terms (that is, those of a loosely protestant cast of mind) were less often in favour of change than those of a more theologically cautious (and arguably Anglican) outlook, a result paralleling the responses on the 'Church' and ecumenism issues.

Just as the social and economic composition of the laity poses problems for the furtherance of the Church's evangelistic mission, the patterns of response and non-response to these attitudinal questions bear witness to additional sources of difficulty. At the most straightforward level, innovation within the Church becomes problematic when active members are divided over the need for change or (as with ecumenism) tend to draw back from institutional action. At a deeper level, for initiatives to be effective they must be legitimated theologically and engage with the 'mental set' of the laity. No doubt clergy have coherent theological views incorporating, *inter alia*, an understanding of the oppositions involved in the division of Western Christianity and in Anglicanism's historical position as a 'bridge' Church. However, although substantial numbers of the laity sampled here appear to have a reasonably secure hold on these same ideas, many others do not. On average over the five issues presented to these respondents, 42 per cent were judged to be unable to operate with the thought structures that underlay the statements presented to them. The point is that it is difficult to lead this particular army, not simply because there are splintering factions with differing war aims, but because some of the more enthusiastic troops lack road-maps, while others have maps but in different editions.

A further feature may be inferred from a certain disparity between the data of this chapter and the last. In respect of the reports from the PCCs, the point was made that in response to the issue of the nature of the Church and how far their own parish measured up to New Testament standards, there was a near absence of any sense of the Church as being the Body of Christ (p. 119). From the survey, however, it transpires that almost everyone endorses precisely this formulation when it is offered to them. The implication is that while this phrase evidently has a prominent place in the 'mantra' of the Church, its implications are sometimes poorly understood and subject to diverse interpretations.

Structures of thought

At this point attention shifts from a consideration of patterns in the religious consciousness of the laity to an exploration of how their religious and secular ideas connect up. This topic arises in an interesting way in relation to the Anglican Church. That the religious and secular are bound up is implied by the nineteenth-century perception of that Church in England and in Wales as 'the Conservative Party at prayer'. No doubt part of the 'reality' behind this remark originates from the distinctive social location of the members of the Church of England. However, since that denomination is an inclusive Church, not an exclusive sect (Troeltsch 1981), Anglicans have always differed among themselves on the full range of political and social issues. Some of these variations are attributable to differences in the social positions of those within the Church. Such locational differences themselves affect religious attitudes, as has already been shown. It is also possible, however, that religious attitudes directly affect secular attitudes. To what extent can religious sources for these variations in secular attitudes be identified?

In order to answer this question, consideration needs to be given not just to the social location of the laity and their religious attitudes but also to their attitudes concerning secular matters. The third section of the questionnaire that was administered to the laity included some questions on social and political issues asked in precisely the same form as that of the *British Social Attitudes* survey (Jowell et al. 1988), so that comparison could be made between the attitudes of 'the faithful' and those of the British people as a whole. Hence, the questionnaire design facilitated an analysis of the structure of religious ideas but also enabled the links between religious and secular attitudes to be explored and interpreted.

Secular attitudes

Once attention moves to the secular sphere, several patterns become evident which reflect the middle-class character of the sample; this is true, for instance, with regard to voting behaviour. Altogether 90 per cent said they had voted at the previous General Election (in 1987), a higher figure than that for the electorate as a whole (75 per cent). The distribution of party support among the respondents was 49 per cent Conservative, 28 per cent Labour, 16 per cent Liberal Democrat, 6 per cent Plaid Cymru (i.e. Welsh Nationalist) and 2 per cent other. Thus, Conservative support was higher than in the UK generally (42.2 per cent) and especially than the Welsh national figure (29.5 per cent), while Labour Party supporters were correspondingly under-represented (UK, 30.8 per cent; Wales, 45.1 per cent; for the national data, see Wood 1987). As expected, support among the respondents for the Liberal Democrat and Welsh Nationalist causes was strongest in the more rural dioceses, and that for the Labour Party in the more urbanized dioceses.

In the questionnaire, the laity were next asked to respond to a number of statements, to elicit their attitudes to certain secular issues. These concerned their view of income inequality in Britain today; which state benefits they felt were too low; whether the problem with welfare benefits was 'scrounging' or a failure to take them up; and whether various groups had too much or too little power. All the questions were such as to enable a direct comparison to be made between the attitudes of respondents and those of the British population as a whole.

Table 7.3   Attitudes to spending on benefits

Type of benefit	% wishing to increase	
	Respondents	British adults
Retirement benefits	64.6	43
Child benefit	28.3	14
Unemployment benefit	23.3	11
Disability benefit	51.7	26
Benefits for single parents	13.8	5

In each case the proportion of respondents favouring an increase was significantly greater than that of British adults as a whole ($p<0.05$).

There was overwhelming support for the view that income inequalities in Britain were too large: 89 per cent of respondents held this view (10 per cent more than in the population as a whole; see Jowell et al. 1988, 216), while 10 per cent felt that they were about right, and only 2 per cent believed they were too small. Various types of welfare benefits serve to reduce some of those inequalities, and Table 7.3 shows the proportion who thought that the government should spend more on each of the main types of benefit. In every case the proportion of the respondents who felt more should be spent was greater than that of the British population as a whole (Jowell et al. 1988, 225). In this respect, therefore, the laity evinced relatively more concern than the British population as a whole for the disadvantaged in society. The respondents were also asked to indicate the benefit that they thought should be given highest priority. Only about half of them felt able to do this, but for those of the laity who did respond the resultant rank order of types of benefit was (1) retirement (cited by 49 per cent); (2) disabled (25 per cent); (3) child (11 per cent); (4) unemployed (10 per cent); and (5) single-parent (2 per cent); with a further 4 per cent asserting that none should have priority. The most obvious conclusion is that the results reflect the concerns of an elderly population.

As regards the use and abuse of benefits, the respondents took a very Anglican position. Yes, they mostly (73 per cent) did think that large numbers of people falsely claimed benefits (compared with 67 per cent of the British population holding this view), but a virtually equal proportion (72 per cent) agreed that large numbers of those eligible for benefits failed to claim them (compared with 83 per cent in the British population; Jowell et al. 1988, 225). Despite their evident 'balance', they were more distrustful of welfare claimants than the British population generally and less concerned about the non-take-up of benefits. It may be that, because of their social characteristics, the laity are less often familiar with actual claimants than the general population, and fewer have experience of the complexities of the benefit system.

Table 7.4 Attitudes to the power of institutions

	Trade unions	Business and industry	Central government	Local government
	%	%	%	%
Too much	48.7	37.1	41.5	21.0
About right	30.2	38.6	35.1	28.3
Too little	6.5	6.3	8.0	30.1
Don't know	14.5	17.8	15.4	20.6
TOTAL	99.9	99.8	100.0	100.0

The respondents were also asked whether they felt that each of four major institutions of society had too much or too little power. In three out of four cases (trade unions, business and industry, and central government) those who felt that the institution exercised too much power considerably outnumbered those who felt that it had too little, but local government provided an exception (Table 7.4). In view of the increase in central government power relative to that of local government in Britain in the preceding years, the figures in the last two columns are not unexpected, although the proportion of the laity who thought that central government had too much power was none the less slightly lower than that in the population as a whole (44 per cent; Jowell et al. 1988, 249). However, while the view that trade unions have too much power was not unreasonable fifteen years earlier, in the eighties their legal and actual power was drastically curbed. Probably because relatively few of the laity are economically active and even fewer belong to unionized occupations, their attitudes seem not to have kept pace with these changes, rather more of them saying that trade unions had too much power than the proportion in the general British population. However, the figure for those respondents who felt that business and industry had too much power was also clearly greater than that in the British population at large (26 per cent; Jowell et al. 1988, 249). In summary, it would seem that among the laity there is a certain sense of powerlessness as against large national 'organizations', both political and economic.

The relationship between religious and secular attitudes

In proceeding to examine the interconnections between these two types of attitudes, it is worth stressing that these data lend themselves to an exploration of the implications in the secular sphere of differences of opinion among Christians on religious questions. Of course, religious issues about which Christians are agreed may well have their own 'secular' implications, but these are more readily demonstrated statistically through a comparison with non-Christian groups. In this case, with respect to each of the five selected religious topics (see appendix to this chapter), there was at least one question which gave rise to a substantial difference of opinion, so one is well placed to identify several differing sources of variation in secular attitudes. (In the data analysis the pair-wise relationship between each religious and each secular variable was examined. In what follows those relationships are described that gave rise to statistically significant patterns of association; chi-square, p<0.05.)

In Set A, opinion was substantially divided between 'catholic', intermediate and 'evangelical' positions as to the nature of the Church. The former religious position emphasizes the authority of the faith and religious traditions. More who took this view identified benefit 'scroungers', and fewer favoured increases in benefits for single parents and the disabled. On this last point, patterns in the data suggest that respondents felt that some of those classified as disabled had made false claims. More generally, worries about 'scroungers' or benefits to single parents suggest the underlying theme of greater sensitivity to breaches of established rules or authority. Interestingly, those agreeing with the 'evangelical' position were also more inclined to identify 'scroungers'. In their case the enhanced sensitivity appears to be towards unconscionable behaviour.

Questions in Set B gave rise to the fewest associations with secular attitude variables. However, those seeing the Church as 'a collection of individuals' more often favoured increasing benefits in relation to children, the disabled and single parents. The underlying pattern would appear to consist in an orientation to the concerns and problems of individuals.

In Set C, concerning changes and the Church, the variable with most secular associations concerned opposition to change within the Church. Those against the Church 'keeping up with the times' also more often identified 'scroungers', more often felt trade union power was excessive (see Table 7.5), and were less often in favour of increased benefits for children and single parents. Three of these items suggest the theme of enhanced concern with the maintenance of (social) stability. On the other hand, the 'radical change' variable was one of only two that correlated with how the respondents voted, agreement being associated with a greater likelihood of a Liberal Democrat or Labour vote. In that case, a linking idea appears to be the rejection of tradition.

Set D included some relatively divisive questions on ecumenism which defined positions for and against, as well as a 'mid' position. Being opposed to ecumenism was associated with an increased likelihood of identifying 'scroungers' and the belief that trade-union power was excessive. Interestingly, agreement with the pro-ecumenism position was also associated with this last belief. The underlying theme is unease in the face of disagreement or conflict, the 'moderates' on this issue being more tolerant of denominational pluralism. On the other hand, it was those who were against ecumenism who evinced most religious certitude (affirming that 'other denominations are wrong'), suggesting a more straightforwardly judgemental approach to law-breaking.

Table 7.5   **Opposition to change in the Church and attitude to trade-union power**

| | | Power of trade unions | | | | |
		Too much	About right	Too little	Total	%
Against change in the Church	Agree	127	48	10	185	35.2
	Mixed feelings	74	42	11	127	24.1
	Disagree	95	98	21	214	40.7
	TOTAL	296	188	42	526	
	%	56.3	35.7	8.0		100.0

(The association of variables was highly significant; chi-square, $p < 0.001$)

Of all the religious variables, the one that most often gave rise to statistically significant patterns of association with secular variables fell in Set E. This set included statements which viewed the world as the object of evangelism, as the object of service, and as intrinsically evil. This last was termed 'world-rejection'. It was the responses to the 'world-rejection' statement that were most associated with secular attitudes. That a variable given this name should have social and political implications is on the face of it less than startling! However, it is worth pointing up that it had significant correlations with responses on many key issues: *viz.* voting behaviour; views on welfare 'scroungers' (see Table 7.6); the power of trade unions, central government and local government; and also whether there should be increases in benefits for children, the unemployed, the disabled and single parents. That this represents something in the way of an opinion 'syndrome' is brought out by the fact that world-rejectors were more likely than others to feel that the powers of both local and central government were excessive, although it would clearly be possible for opinions in these matters to go in opposite directions.

It is instructive to examine patterns in the data from an alternative viewpoint and inquire as to which secular attitudes had fewest, and which had most, religious correlates. The only secular variable with no religious correlates was 'benefits for the retired'. This being a predominantly elderly sample, it is hard to

Table 7.6   'World-rejection' and the identification of 'scroungers'

| | 'Large numbers falsely claim benefits' | | | | |
	Agree	Mixed feelings	Disagree	Total	%
Attitude of world-rejection					
Agree	176	59	12	247	38.5
Mixed feelings	118	54	23	195	30.4
Disagree	112	53	25	200	31.2
TOTAL	406	166	70	642	
%	63.2	25.9	10.9		100.0

(The association of variables was highly significant; chi-square $p<0.001$)

avoid the inference that the niceties of 'theological differences' within a group become altogether less salient in relation to the interests of its own members.

By contrast, the secular matter with most religious correlates was the identification of 'scroungers', and this was followed by the issues of benefits for the disabled, the power of trade unions, and benefits for single parents. Certainly, some of these items are commonly viewed as 'emotive' issues, but it is worth dwelling on what else differentiates these variables from others. It can be suggested that a focal concern from a religious viewpoint is that of responsibility and, where appropriate, blame; the issues where religiously defined groups differ most in their opinions are those that can be most readily analysed in this respect. 'Scroungers' are responsible for their (possibly wrong) actions; by contrast, the disabled are viewed as unfortunate, as (in general) not having willed their condition (although those seeking to benefit from being falsely so classified are culpable). Again, trade unions are seen as being responsible for their actions, as (in general) single parents are for their state. There is a contrast, for instance, with the situation of the unemployed, who may or may not be viewed as responsible for their condition.

Taking a position on theological issues entails a refinement of thinking which expresses itself in secular terms through modifications in the judgements of events and situations where responsibility and blame may be allocated. Although there will be resultant modifications of judgement in relation to situations both straightforward and complex, they are evidently more readily detected in a (concomitant variation) investigation, such as this, in contexts which are straightforward in the sense indicated. A 'simple' example demonstrating a movement of thought in the opposite direction (from the secular to the religious) is provided by the parable of the woman taken in adultery. She is (straightforwardly) responsible for her own actions, but we are being invited to draw back from an immediate condemnatory judgement and, through deeper consideration, to elaborate our response: therein lies the theological lesson. Once the religious point of the parable has been absorbed, modifications in judgement should be evident across a range of 'secular' instances.

Interests and religious values

It seems reasonable to interpret these data on secular attitudes as reflecting in part the economic and social position that the laity occupy, and in part their religious beliefs. For instance, their general views on benefits seemed to demonstrate the 'bias to the poor' that David Sheppard, when Bishop of Liverpool, affirmed to be associated with the Christian Gospel; but in focusing particularly on retirement benefits, they gave more direct expression to the interests of an elderly population. The outlook on trade unionism seemed dated, and demonstrative of a lack of familiarity with recent changes affecting industrial power relations. Their views both in this respect and on welfare claimants point up the limitations placed on the laity as a whole by their concentration in certain social locations in a way that renders them unrepresentative of the population as a whole. A further detectable pattern was for the laity, as individuals, to experience a sense of powerlessness in the face of large national 'organizations', whether political or economic (or both), and to feel that the main influence they themselves had was at a local level. It may well be that a tendency to feel impotent in the face of large social and economic forces (clearly shared with many in the general population) is related to a strongly local orientation arising from long residence in the same place.

As far as links between the two types of attitudes are

concerned, differences of opinion on each of the five selected religious topics seemed to have identifiable implications in the secular sphere. As regards differing positions as to the nature of the Church, those with 'catholic' views seemed more oriented in their secular judgements to rule-breaking or a challenge to authority, while 'evangelicals' reacted more strongly to that which could be viewed as unconscionable behaviour (thereby sometimes arriving at the same conclusion by different routes). Again, an 'Anglican individualist' conception of Church structure can be associated with enhanced sensitivity to individual, as opposed to group, interests. From a consideration of views on change, two further linked ideas expressed in a religious context could be seen to have secular implications: the maintenance of stability, and the preparedness or otherwise to abandon tradition. A focus on ecumenism suggests that a further dimension of religious attitudes is concerned with the toleration or rejection of pluralism and moral relativities. Finally, but particularly influential in its secular implications, is the presence or absence of the attitude termed here 'world-rejection'. It also seems that the secular issues on which religiously defined groups differ most in their opinions are those that can be most readily analysed in terms of responsibility and blame.

Appendix
The Fifteen Religious-Attitude Statements
(grouped as presented in the text of this chapter)

Respondents were asked to indicate the extent of their agreement or disagreement:

Set A: concerning the 'nature' of the Church

A1	A2	A3
The trouble with the Church today is that it is full of people who are unwilling to accept the authority of the Christian faith and the traditions of the Church and the use of the sacraments as a means of growth in personal holiness.	The trouble with the Church today is that it includes two groups: one lot over-emphasizes tradition, authority and the Church, and the other lot overemphasizes personal experience and the individual. Our job as Anglicans is to get the balance right.	The trouble with the Church today is that it is full of people whose lives are not based on a personal relationship with Jesus, and who are afraid to live their lives in the power of the Holy Spirit.
'catholic'	'*via media*'	'evangelical'

Set B: concerning the 'structure' of the Church

B1	B2	B3
The Church is not just a set of individuals, or a collection of parishes, but the Body of Christ, the means by which Christ is active in the human world.	We hear far too much today about Church bodies and organizations. These are at best a necessary evil and at worst a positive hindrance to the real life of the Church: the life of the local worshipping community led by its clergy.	We hear far too much today about Church bodies and organizations. These are not the Church. The Church is simply a fellowship of all those who have accepted Jesus as their Lord and Saviour.
'sacramental'	'congregational'	'individualist'

Set C: concerning change and the Church

C1	C2	C3
The trouble with the Church today is that it keeps changing to keep up with the times. It should be the one thing that stays the same.	What people in the Church today cannot grasp is that because the world around us is changing the Church has to change if it is to preach effectively the unchanging Gospel of Jesus Christ.	The trouble with the Church today is that it is imprisoned in the past. It needs to have the courage to reject its traditions so that it can become free to witness effectively to the Gospel.
'conservative'	'moderate'	'radical'

Set D: concerning the ecumenical movement

D1	D2	D3
I am Anglican because I believe other denominations are wrong. I look forward to the day when the traditional Churches are reformed and the Nonconformist denominations return to their Mother Church.	I accept that members of other Churches and denominations are just as much Christians as we are; I believe we should be partners, not enemies, in spite of our differences; but frankly *I think that Covenanting and Councils of Churches and other ecumenical activities are a complete waste of time and effort.*	Tolerance and understanding between members of Churches and organizations are not enough. Our divisions are a scandal, and all Christians should spare no effort to create a single Christian Church in this country.
'opposed'	'opposed to institutional unity'	'favourable'

Set E: concerning the Church and the world

E1	E2	E3
Some people think that the Church should spend its time doing things for people outside it. That point of view turns Christians into do-gooders, and the clergy into social workers. The job of the Church is to worship God and fight against the world outside the Church.	The job of the Church is to go out into the world and preach the Good News of Jesus Christ.	The job of the Church is to witness to the love of God for His Creation by serving and caring for His children, wherever and whoever they may be.
'world-rejecting' (world as evil)	'world-accepting', 1 (world as the object of evangelism)	'world-accepting', 2 (world as the object of Christian service)

Part Three

*Religious witness in a
postmodern culture*

8

A post-establishment church in a postmodern society

The first chapter of this book defined the situation of the Church in Wales as that of a post-establishment church in a secular society. This definition involved the recognition that the Church in Wales is committed to maintaining its presence throughout Wales and defines its mission as the spiritual care of all those resident in its dioceses who are not of non-Christian faiths and not adherents of other Christian Churches, and that the viability of this mission is threatened by the increasing secularization of the society of which it is part.

To say that we live in an increasingly secular society is in no way inconsistent with the claim that in every society and in every age individuals have 'spiritual' needs which are supplied in and through association with others. It is not even inconsistent with the claim, a discussion of whose validity lies outside the scope of this study, that the nineties have been a period in which, among the members of the population outside the main Christian Churches, there is a growing awareness of the existence of spiritual needs and a certain casting-about to supply them. To say that we live in a secular society is to say that religious faiths and institutions have lost their hegemonic domination. Christianity is no longer a faith one opts out of but a faith which one has to opt for. One no longer has to have a reason for not practising Christianity, but a reason for starting, or, for those with a Christian upbringing, a reason for continuing.

It is sometimes said that, as a result of secularization, the Churches now find themselves in a position similar to that of the early Church. There is an element of truth in this claim, but only an element. Granted, the ancient world, like the contemporary world, was not Christian. It was, however, not secular but pagan. People worshipped gods, and St Paul was able to say to the

Greeks, before their altar to 'the unknown God': 'whom you have worshipped in ignorance, Him I proclaim unto you'. There is no contemporary equivalent. While the human propensity for idolatry may be regarded as a constant (outside a utopia in which human alienation has finally been abolished), in contemporary society the pursuit of unlimited wealth (for example) takes a secular and not a religious form. The Stock Exchange does not preface its proceedings with libations to Mammon.

In these circumstances, maintaining the Anglican form of Christian witness in every locality within its territory is itself problematic, and transforming the life of local Anglican communities from one oriented to mission rather than maintenance is a task of considerable difficulty. Yet the possession of a territorial organization, together with the existence of central funds which contribute towards its maintenance, provides the Anglican Church in Wales with a unique opportunity.

The first part of this book has, therefore, been concerned with the Church in Wales as a territorial organization. The substantive problems faced by the Church are discussed as they appear in organizational *forms*. The second part of the book is concerned with the *content* of those forms: namely, the life of the benefices in which the Anglican people of God, clerical and lay, are gathered, and without which there would be nothing to organize. The view from the parishes of the Church is, in organizational terms, the view from the 'bottom up' rather than from the 'top down'. Part Two was, however, primarily concerned not with the organizational aspect of the Church but with the character, attitudes and activities of the people whom it comprises. In this way we have attempted to provide a rounded sociological picture of a major church.

In Part Three we attempt to widen the perspective in which the situation of the Church may be understood. Had resources permitted, we would have enlarged the study to include data on the religious attitudes of those outside the Christian Churches, so as to locate the attitudes of Church members within contemporary culture. Instead we shall argue that the difficulties faced by Church members with their faith and practice cannot adequately be grasped through the characterization of that culture as 'secular', but are of a kind more generally confronted by the inhabitants of societies having a culture which has been termed 'postmodern'.

The problems of post-establishment

To say that the Church in Wales is a post-established church is to make two claims. First, it is to claim that it is a church to which the members of the Welsh population no longer feel they have a duty to belong, but one to which they none the less have a right to belong; in consequence, the Church has a duty to serve that population. Its post-establishment status is evidenced by the lack of coincidence between the categories formed by those who receive Communion at Easter and those who communicate regularly. Those communicating only at Easter (and other major festivals) may be thought of as a survival from the days of establishment; their attendance at Easter is a ritual recognition of their inherited membership of a Christian society and its Church. They are a survival from the days when society rather than the individual was religious, and religious participation was a matter of social obligation rather than personal commitment.

Some part of the fall in ECs is, therefore, a sign of the increasing secularization of society rather than of a decline in individual religiosity. That this is so is evidenced by the analysis of benefice characteristics in Chapter 4, which distinguished two clusters of variables, ecclesiastical and secular, variations in the number of ECs being associated not with variations in the ecclesiastical, but with the secular, variables. Chief of these were the size and density of benefice populations. The 'Easter only' category is more marked in rural areas of Wales, while in more urban areas the numbers of Easter and weekly communicants are closer. It follows that the current annual fall in ECs is a result, in part, of the increasing secularization of the countryside. The implications for the Church of this decline are none the less serious. An established church is by definition one which is open to the society within which it is set. The 'Easter only' category constitutes a bridge between those wholly outside the Church and those committed to it. The erosion of this category, therefore, constitutes a movement by the Church away from the character of an *ecclesia* towards that of a 'denomination'. It also represents a reduction in the opportunities for mission, not in the sense of converting the heathen but in the sense of increasing the numbers of committed members of the Church.

To say that the Church in Wales is a post-establishment church is also to claim that, though in many respects it is becoming, sociologically, more like a 'denomination' than an *ecclesia*, its structure and the assumptions that underpin it are still those of an established church in a Christian society. This structure is territorial. The central problem of a post-establishment church is the maintenance of a comprehensive territorial structure under social conditions which are quite different from those under which the structure originated.

While the 'order' of the Church (the hierarchy of bishops, priests and deacons) is normative, not instrumental, its territorial organization arose and persisted because it was an effective means to the Church's normative ends. While the Church's order is not to be judged in terms of its effectiveness, therefore, considerations of effectiveness do apply to its territorial organization. However, because that organization arose naturally and was not purposively designed, and has been handed down from generation to generation, it has come to be traditionally legitimated. Though it is not, theologically, a matter of 'order', it is none the less, sociologically, part of the normative order of the Church and therefore is not regarded as a means whose appropriateness depends on the conditions under which the Church has to act. As a result, it has one of the features of traditionally legitimated organizational forms: there is no specific means for evaluating its effectiveness and instituting change in its territorial organization.

While the Church can alter its diocesan boundaries, there is no organizational means whereby it can monitor their appropriateness, short of setting up a special commission to do so. Equally, dioceses have no regular means of reviewing the effectiveness of their parochial organization. Nor is there any means of ensuring that the distribution of resources (clergy and money) between dioceses is appropriate to the priorities the Church assigns to the achievement of different goals. This is not surprising, because there is no institutional procedure for defining goals, and no culture of evaluating the traditional organization (and the consequent resource distribution) in terms of changing priorities. As a result, at both provincial and diocesan levels, the Church in Wales is, in the judgement of one informant, 'excellent at producing reports, but very poor at acting upon them'.

Chapter 3 demonstrated the diversity of the six dioceses of the Province on a number of dimensions. Attempts to create dioceses in which urban and rural, and rich and poor, areas are balanced, have been frustrated by the complexity of Welsh social and economic geography. Of central importance in organizational terms is the inequality of dioceses in terms of resources, especially money and clergy. The inequality of dioceses can be measured in terms of the ratio of a given resource to the numbers of population, or of ECs, or of weekly congregation. It was one of the conclusions of that chapter that the distribution of clergy between dioceses is appropriate to the attainment of the objective of pastoral care of existing congregations, but not to enlarging those congregations by bringing in those outside the Church or to bringing occasional communicants into active membership. Dioceses are unequal in respect of clergy distribution in relation to the attainment of each of the latter two objectives, each of which requires a different distribution. However, even if there were mechanisms for determining priorities between the different objectives, there is no means by which the Church's Governing Body could effect them, since the dioceses are responsible for staffing and funding their own parishes, and the only existing central role is that of the Representative Body in providing what are in effect grants-in-aid to the dioceses. However, that body is only concerned with the management of the Church's property and finances, not with the manner in which the sums it makes available are disbursed by the dioceses.

Sociologically, the Church, even in a secular society, is always part of society, since its members occupy statuses and perform roles which are part of the structure of that society, in addition to those that belong to the social structure of the Church. The analysis of benefices' characteristics in Chapter 4 treated the benefice as being part of its locality, and as having, therefore, both secular and ecclesiastical characteristics. Among twenty-four variables which that analysis employed it was possible to distinguish those that were the properties of the religious group and those that were the properties of the local society of which the religious group was part.

There are two possible, opposing views of the relation between the religious and the secular thus conceived, which are themselves religious and secular. The religious view is that the religious characteristics of a religious group are spiritually determined; the secular view is that religious characteristics must be treated in the same way as any other social attribute. The latter view is espoused by some sociologists of religion who preach the doctrine of 'methodological atheism'. We regard this view as secularist rather than sociological. Sociologically the distinction is not between the religious and the secular but between action and structure or, alternatively, between belief and action and the conditions of action. To put it yet another way, those characteristics of religious groups that are the result of the actions and convictions of their members have to be understood as responses to the social situations in which they find themselves. Those actions and convictions will therefore tend to change as the social conditions change. However, the nature of the response to changed conditions is not uniquely determined by them. Congregations in benefices with the same social conditions may respond to them in different ways, and the same types of change may evoke different responses in different benefices. This approach would lead us to expect that the actions of religious groups would show a degree of autonomy relative to the secular conditions under which their members have to act.

That this understanding is correct is suggested by the fact that the analysis of benefice variables in Chapter 4 shows the existence of two separate, clusters of closely related variables, one secular and one ecclesiastical, with no strong relations between them. Four variables emerge as particularly salient indicators, two being secular and two ecclesiastical. The ratio of ECs to the local population size correlates with secular variables and appears, therefore, to indicate the level of secularization of the local 'society' of which the religious group is a part. By contrast, measures of lay commitment and lay participation generally lack associations with secular variables, and higher values can therefore more appropriately be taken to imply 'successful' action on behalf of the members of the religious group.

There is, therefore, from a sociological point of view, nothing inevitable about the decline of religious practice in the face of an increasingly secularized society. That depends on how people react to the change in the conditions of their action which increasing secularization implies. However, there are conditions of their action other than those imposed by a changing society, and those conditions are those constituted by the character of the religious organization of which they are part; they are those of a post-established church which has retained a parochial system which evolved to suit the conditions of an established church in a religious society. The paradox here is that the strength of the Church lies not in its organization but in its parishes, and any attempt to replace the parochial by some other form of territorial organization could destroy the foundation of the allegiance of its most faithful members. However, the Church in Wales needs to become at least able to consider a modification of its traditional form of territorial organization, and to regard it as a humanly devised means to fulfil its mission rather than as an end in itself, if the Church is to respond effectively to the challenges of the twenty-first century.

The clergy–laity relation

The movement from a consideration of ecclesiastical organization in Part One to a consideration of clergy and people in Part Two, involved a shift of focus onto the living social groups that are the social basis and foundation of the Church and in comparison with which super-ordinate bodies are mere superstructure. The reason that this is so is to be found in the nature of the Church's 'order', which is based on a single fundamental relationship: that between priest and people, whether that relationship takes the form of a priest having the oversight of other priests and their people – as in the case of a bishop – or whether that oversight is confined to that of the laity – as in the case of the parochial clergy. No such relationship pertains at the provincial level: archbishops *qua arch*bishops do not share the cure of the souls of the inhabitants of their province with its clergy. It is the absence of this fundamental role in their capacity purely as *arch*bishops that has led to the custom of Anglican archbishops being always simultaneously bishops of a diocese.

Part One has described a church in a state of 'crisis' (in that sense of the word which means both 'difficulty' and 'challenge') which has arisen as a result of rapid social change and throws into question traditional forms of ecclesiastical organization. However, for those who are in one sense nearer the site of contemporary social change, the parochial clergy, the crisis occurred some time ago. In the late sixties, a parish in the Llŷn Peninsula told its bishop that 'the days when the parson lived in a big house, had an income of a thousand a year and was looked up to and feared by the people of the village have long gone'. The declining wealth and social status of the Anglican clergy over the last hundred years, their loss of the automatic right to exercise local leadership, combined in Wales with the Anglican Church's disestablishment, meant that the traditional social role of the clergy was thrown into crisis long before the arrival of the crisis now experienced by the 'Church-as-organization'. And yet the 'order' of the Church was not changed. Incumbents were still priests charged with the cure of souls of the inhabitants of their parish or group of parishes. It was the secular world around them that had changed, requiring that they discharge their sacred function under different social (secular) conditions.

If a distinction be made between the sacred and profane aspects (Durkheim 1961) of the Anglican clergy role, then it may be said that clergy experienced a crisis in that they lost the profane aspects of their role at a time when the population they served was showing a decreasing concern for the sacred. However, this is too simplistic a way of putting the matter, since it confuses the line between the Church and its social environment with the sacred/profane distinction. Clergy have lost their previous status in the profane world constituted by the social environment of their religious group, but they still occupy *a* status within the profane world – a much lower one. This loss of status was of peculiar importance in the case of an established church, since a parish priest charged with the care of the whole population of his parish requires status and authority *vis-à-vis* the members of that population, not just in relation to members of his congregation. The adequate performance of the sacred role of parish priest requires, as a means, an appropriate status in the profane world. Conversely, the life of a religious group requires material resources which have to be managed, and demands of clergy the performance of administrative tasks which lie on the profane side of the sacred/profane divide but are none the less incumbent upon the clergy by virtue of their sacred calling. The sacred/profane division does not, therefore, follow the division between the religious group and the secular world but, rather, refers to aspects of the clergy's status in both social spheres. Anglican parish priests occupy a distinctive social situation as a consequence of their institutionally specified ministry to the world outside the gathered congregation of the faithful, deriving, in the case of the Church in Wales, from its post-establishment character.

It is against this background that the evidence of Chapter 5 concerning what clergy do and what they feel about their different activities must be interpreted. A joint consideration of the responses regarding time pressure leads to the conclusion that the components of their occupational role that clergy tend to conceptualize as absorbing too much time tend to be profane activities, and those components for which they feel they have insufficient time are unambiguously 'sacred' activities. At the same time, the demands of their occupational role as a whole are seen as leaving too little time for their personal life. It may be that the existence of the profane category within the occupational role obviates the necessity for the recognition of any direct conflict between either personal self-interest or personal moral responsibilities and the duties of their vocation. The erosion of leisure and (even) the occurrence of moral conflict associated with the clergy role are blamed upon the profane rather than upon the sacred components of the occupational role.

The division of clergy concerns into personal, sacred and profane shows marked similarities to that devised by Blizzard (1985) in his study of the Protestant parish minister. In a chapter on role conflict, that author distinguishes between the personal and the occupational and between the traditional and the contemporary aspects of the minister's role. Conflict was most frequently reported between the personal–traditional and occupational–contemporary segments and between the traditional–occupational and the contemporary–occupational segments. The first of these conflicts corresponds to what was termed in Chapter 5 the 'squeezing' of the personal life of the minister by the intrusion of profane occupational concerns, while the second represents a direct conflict within the occupational segment between the sacred and the profane. Blizzard sums up this latter distinction as being between, on the one hand, the minister as preacher, priest, teacher, and pastor and, on the other, the minister as organizer and administrator.

This interpretation goes some way to explaining the most obvious and striking aspect of the results: the strong adherence shown by the clergy to the traditional definition of their role. Clergy are deeply wedded to their traditional activities of visiting, study and the conducting of services, hostile to attempts to get them to change their ways, tired of having their work interrupted by what they conceive of as endless meetings and the filling of forms sent out by ecclesiastical bureaucrats. Their complaints were evidence of an alienation between the clergy and ecclesiastical administrators, based on a normative belief in the intrinsic nature of the clergy's vocation, which they felt they were being asked to violate. At the same time, the new demands being made were inconsistent with their own motivations on entering the ministry. They had sought to perform their traditional role out of a sense of vocation and because that was what they felt able to do well. However, the rapid secularization of society shifts the emphasis of the Church as organization from a pastoral ministry (service provision) to an evangelical ministry (service extension), transforming the traditional role of clergy. Clergy sometimes complained of the attitudes of the laity in being resistant to change and over-reliant on priestly leadership. The clergy perhaps failed to recognize, however, that the adoption of less conservative attitudes by others would necessitate a change in their own role, which would reveal the clergy to be as conservative, though in different ways, as those of whom they complained.

Relevant evidence on this point was provided by a consideration of relationships between the four general attitude variables, which suggested a tendency among some clergy almost to equate the religious situation in Wales with that of their own Church. This is an important finding with respect to the capability of the Church for mission, given that Wales is a society in which, traditionally, the majority of the population in many areas has had allegiance to other denominations. An appreciation of the 'missionary situation' in any area must take into account the relative strengths of all the Christian denominations. Hence, in Wales it is vital that missionary outreach be ecumenical in approach. The tendency of Anglican clergy to see the missionary situation in Wales primarily in Anglican terms does not bode well for the Church's future evangelistic effectiveness.

The picture that emerges from the evidence of Chapter 5 is of clergy accentuating the sacred/profane divide within the religious group, identifying strongly with its sacred as opposed to its profane aspects, the latter being conceived of as the concern of lay Church members. However, we believe the distinction

between the sacred and the profane is not one which is, in practice, helpful to the Christian *laos*; nor is it helpful sociologically in
defining religious phenomena, which was the role assigned to it
by Durkheim. The Anglican Church rightly describes the
ministry of its clergy as the 'Sacred Ministry'. Prefacing the term
'ministry' with the adjective 'sacred' presupposes other Christian
ministries and vocations which are not 'set apart', as Durkheim
put it. The Church in its *terminology*, therefore, uses the
Durkheimian distinction to distinguish between different sub-
classes of phenomena of the same kind (Christian ministries), not
between classes of phenomena of different kinds (religious/spiri-
tual and secular ministries). There is a tendency, however, for
both clergy and laity, like Durkheim, to confuse the sacred with
the religious, with the result that a false distinction is made by
clergy between different elements within their vocational role
and, within the Christian community, between the respective
roles of clergy and of laity, giving the clergy a monopoly of the
religious and relegating the role of the laity to a concern with
the secular. The clergy role is indeed sacred, and for a good
Durkheimian reason; namely, because clergy represent a social
totality, not because they have a monopoly of the religious/
spiritual.

Chapters 6 and 7 are concerned with the laity. Chapter 6
describes the views of the laity as articulated by a sample of
PCCs. These data necessarily have three aspects: the religious,
the material and the social. It is our view that what is thereby
revealed is basic to the issue of the Church's survival, the first
being the more fundamental. The first has to do with the capacity of the laity to witness to the faith they have received, the last
is concerned with the practical steps being taken to make this
witness effective. However, the religious is simultaneously social:
from religious belief flows the formation of worshipping communities, and from the witness to those beliefs flow relationships
with non-believers. In addition, both these activities require
material resources which have to be managed.

Although the laity are aware that there are frequently too many
church buildings and that many are wrongly positioned, they are
not over-worried by the associated administrative burden which
this imposes on the clergy or by the drain that they impose on a
parish's financial resources. There is clearly a need for more

effective dissemination of information to ensure an accurate understanding of the way in which parishes are funded. More fundamentally, administrative responsibilities need to be reviewed and consciously allocated, a need dramatically evidenced by the fact that one-third of parishes were unable to answer a question about the pattern of clergy activities since they confessed to ignorance of what they were. As far as finance is concerned, an urgent requirement is the specification of realistic guidelines for personal giving. However, the nature of lay responsibilities in these overtly material matters is simultaneously spiritual and social in character and can only be clarified by reference to the Church's theology.

To insist on the necessity of theologically interpreting and evaluating religious practice is not to intellectualize and despiritualize religious practice and experience or to claim that salvation in the Christian or Anglican tradition is dependent on the intellectual orthodoxy of a person's belief. However, to claim to be a Christian in the Anglican tradition is to give assent to a set of beliefs and understandings about the nature of the world, God and the Church, and in so far as a person's religious practice is inconsistent with those basic beliefs they cannot be said to be Anglican. In the modern age, people have learned to accept the authority of the specialist, the expert; and the distinctiveness of the clergy lies, for many of the laity, in their theological training rather than their priestly status. This means that, in St Paul's words, 'giving a reason for the faith that is within us' is often regarded as something that can safely be left to those who are, from the point of view of the laity in the parishes, the local theological experts: the parochial clergy. The point, however, is that the very existence of the Church, as a community of believers, requires that its members have a common consciousness both of the Gospel to which it witnesses and of its nature as a divine institution as understood in the Anglican tradition. This is not to require that all lay members be specialist theologians, but it is to ask them to seek to make sense of, and shape, their individual lives and relationships and that of the collectivity of the Church in Christian terms. A comprehensive failure to do so would signal the end of the Christian community as surely as would its total loss of membership. In this regard, the notion of the Church as a community of believers bears a certain comparison with the notion of a genuine democracy: it is necessary in each context not simply for individual members to know that this is the case but for their lives to be informed in broad terms by the implications. A significant teaching task faces the Church as it seeks to disseminate a better lay understanding of such theological conceptions as the Church as the Body of Christ, the Christian understanding of vocation and ministry, and Christian stewardship, since these understandings have a profound effect on the way in which, in the parishes, scarce resources are administered and parochial activities distributed between lay and clerical members.

The Church is a traditional organization inasmuch as its task is not to innovate but to hand down the faith to every new generation so that it may be preached anew. Max Weber wrote that 'the task of the cultural sciences must be begun anew in every age'. Weber was referring primarily to the practice of historiography, which he saw as bridging the gap between a continually changing present and a fixed past. A religion faces, culturally, the same problem – that of translating a set of understandings originating in the past into terms which are those of the culture of the 'age' in which it finds itself. It was clear from the responses of the parishes that the laity are being left to accomplish this task largely on their own, since some of them complain of the meaningless of much traditional religious language in which the Gospel is currently couched. The collapse of the traditional language in which timeless theological truths are expressed requires of the laity a better theological understanding than was needed previously. That is only one step to the solution of the problem, however. Once understood, these theological principles then need to be applied creatively in such a way that they can inform Christian practice not only within Christian communities but in the secular world.

The Church is, however, a traditional organization in a more profound sense: the beliefs and social practices that constitute it are legitimated by reference to tradition. Yet it is one of the characteristics of post-modern society that tradition has lost its legitimating function. 'Tradition more and more must be contemplated, defended, sifted through, in relation to an awareness that there exists a variety of other ways of doing things' (Giddens 1994, 83). The shift from the unquestioning acceptance of tradition to its examination and the consequent loss of its legitimating power has led Giddens to describe contemporary society as being in the process of 'detraditionalization'.

Nowhere were the problems of the relation between the Church and contemporary society more clearly evidenced than in the concern of parochial church councils with worship. Two different types of problem emerged. The first concerned the challenge posed by the complex structure of contemporary society: that is to say, by the fact that it is made up of a large number of very different groups and categories. While this obviously poses problems for the Church's Liturgical Commission in devising forms of service which suit such a wide range of participants, what is striking is that parishes, within which social differentiation must be far less great than that in Wales as a whole, perceived themselves to be in this sort of difficulty to so great an extent that they felt it necessary to offer a whole range of different types of services if they were to supply the needs of their local populations.

The second problem concerned the changing culture of contemporary society, which in many respects is alien to the culture of the Anglican Communion. The opposition here is not between the religious and the secular or between the Christian and the pagan. It is not the secularity of contemporary culture that creates the problem but its style. For example, those young people who frequent concerts of popular music would be as out of place at an evening of community singing, be it never so secular, as at Solemn Evensong. Anglican worship involves thinking and reflection; the spiritual and emotional are integrated with the intellectual in a way which makes more difficult the formulation of a response to charismatic and other rival evangelical movements, whose style of worship is far from providing a space in which those who are 'wearied by the changes and chances of this fleeting world may repose upon [God's] eternal changelessness'. While few respondents specifically identified such movements as constituting a challenge to which the Anglican Church had to respond, the wide concern of the parishes with the form and content as well as with the pattern of services included frequent recognition that contemporary Anglican worship lacked something that more demonstrative forms of worship supplied.

What was lacking was rarely defined, but some parishes identified it as the lack of the expression of joy; congregations were not fired by an infectious enthusiasm. Joy is, however, a gift of the

Holy Spirit, and that Spirit manifested itself in tongues of fire. In their identification of something wanting in contemporary Anglican worship, the parishes were recognizing the absence of something that can only be expressed in theological and Trinitarian terms: namely, that traditionally the Church has worshipped the Father through the Son, but in common with other denominations, has placed much less emphasis on the Spirit. The *Veni, Creator Spiritus* plays little part in Anglican liturgy. Only once a year do the faithful sing 'Come Holy Ghost our souls inspire', and most parishes would be rather embarrassed if that prayer was answered.

This problem is simultaneously cultural and theological. When asked about the nature of the Church, the parishes' responses revealed an absence of concern with the Holy Spirit. The Church, the parishes rightly said, is a fellowship of believers, but there was little sense that what makes a fellowship part of the Christian Church is the in-dwelling of the Holy Spirit. As in worship, God is 'out there', Father–Creator, risen and ascended Lord, but not 'God with us'. This absence of a proper understanding of the relations between Church and Spirit has practical implications for the relation between clergy and laity. According to Anglican theology, all Church members receive the Holy Spirit (in baptism and confirmation). According to St Paul, all Christians are 'called' to be saints. It follows that all members of the *laos*, not just the clergy, have 'religious' vocations and the grace to follow them. However, the laity, like the clergy, made a radical distinction between the functions of clergy and of laity, seeing it as inappropriate for the laity to assist their parish priest in 'his' sacred duties, and only feeling called to tasks which were coded as profane. The problems of the relationship between clergy and laity and of the relation between the worshipping congregation and the general population in respect of worship are both rooted in this inadequate understanding of the role of the Spirit in the life of the Christian community.

Culturally, the coldness and formality of the Anglican liturgy and its musical style are in direct contrast to the style of secular congregations of younger people, where public performances are designed to create ecstatic states leading to the transcendence of individuality. However, worship more in tune with current cultural forms would, if imported wholesale, immediately destroy the balance of elements which is the hallmark of Anglicanism. This is one of several identifiable areas where the Church will encounter one set of difficulties if it changes, and another if it does not – a dilemma which can no longer be resolved by reference to the authority of tradition.

The Church and society

So far this discussion has concentrated on what goes on 'inside' the Church, but in spite of that focus we have been forced to begin to consider the relation between the Church and the society in which it is set. In turning to examine, as in Chapter 7, the characteristics of the laity and their religious and social attitudes, the focus shifts to a consideration of the relation between the two types of attitude and thus to a consideration of the Church as a part of society.

One of the conclusions of Chapter 7 is that large numbers of the laity seem unable to operate with thought structures in whose terms the distinctive character of Anglican Christianity has been defined. These thought structures largely depend on the opposition of the Catholic and Protestant versions of the Christian faith, between which Anglicanism has sought to provide a *via media*. Since the division of the Western Church into Catholic and Protestant is associated with the commencement of the 'modern' era, it is legitimate to regard that division, and the Anglican response to it, as distinctive features of modernity in the religious sphere. In the case of three of the issues presented in the survey of the laity, the majority of the response patterns make sense in the context of the theological oppositions involved in the Catholic/Protestant division. However, the thought patterns of a large minority of lay people did not correspond to the ideal typical oppositions of religious modernity. None the less, their ability to respond to the language employed in those attitude statements attests to the extent to which the laity are, so to speak, children of modernity. The existence both of a traditionally modern majority and of a minority for whom modern signifiers still operate but no longer in the modern way suggests that the collective consciousness of the laity of the Church in Wales, so far from being opposed to that of contemporary society is very much part of it, in the sense that both are clearly 'postmodern'. The

Church finds itself in a situation which is characteristically post-modern in this sense: the structures of religious modernity still discernibly operate, but they have lost their hegemonic dominance without that dominance being challenged by any identifiable alternative.

To tie the current problems of a Church to those of a *postmodern* society and culture is, however, to do more than characterize the consciousness of the laity in this way. The period of greatest social and cultural change in recent history was that of the Industrial Revolution. But by the completion of the first cycle of that monumental change, the outlines of the new society that was coming into being were already discernible, even if their implications were not fully understood. Moreover, the very concepts through which its nature could be grasped had already been formed. The alternative to an agrarian society was, that is to say, already identifiable. To find a parallel to our present situation, however, it is necessary to go back to the birth of modernity itself, to the period of the Reformation, when the problems of the new type of society and the new type of religious consciousness that was then coming into being were still conceived of in medieval terms. What is now called the 'early modern' period could, we suggest, be thought of as analogous to that of the second half of the twentieth century and denominated as 'post-medieval'.

Unless the radical nature of the changes that are now overtaking society and culture is recognized, they can be misidentified as merely yet another stage in the process of rapid change characteristic of modernity itself. Here an analogy suggests itself between the present condition of the Church and those recently experienced by each of the major British political parties: Labour in the early eighties, and the Conservative Party in the late nineties. Faced with electoral disaster, both parties interpreted their task as 'modernization': that is, catching up with the change in the society of which they were part in terms of both organization and ideology. In the parties, as in the Churches, there are bands of 'faithful' adherents who both believe and practice. However, survival in both spheres requires that the 'faithful' go out and win new adherents from social groups other than those from which their supporters have traditionally been drawn. Both have problems centrally concerned either with what their faith is (the political parties) or the categories through which it is expressed (the Church). However, in spite of the fact that the traditional categories are inadequate under contemporary circumstances, neither is able to abandon them without falling into incoherence. Both types of institution face a massive task of (re-)education if their fundamental principles are to be once again understood; yet, in the application of those principles, each has got to be willing to listen as well as to teach if its message is to survive in the postmodern age. Thus, listening is necessary not merely to enable the dressing-up of traditional beliefs and practices in new clothes which make them meaningful to the members of contemporary society; it is also necessary if traditional principles are to be applied to new and rapidly changing circumstances. At the time of writing, spring 1998, the electoral victory of New Labour has been widely welcomed, but the ensuing debate concerning the cost of the victory serves to focus the dilemma of the Church. Has Labour's success been achieved at the cost of coming to resemble the enemy? Has 'modernization' meant that the anchor of principle has been broken/raised, leaving the ship floating directionless in potentially stormy seas, its crew concerned only with keeping afloat? To preach its gospel successfully, any radical political party must, like the Church, be in the world but not of it. Here, however, the analogy ends, for the *raison d'être* of any political party is winning political power, while the Church's mission is to preach its gospel 'whether they hear or whether they forbear'. As a consequence, Churches are less prone than parties to 'run after every new thing' (modernize) in their pursuit of adherents. The vice corresponding to this virtue is that they may concentrate so much on not being 'of' the world that they may end up not being 'in' it. One of the forces driving change in political groupings – the will to power – is therefore absent from the Church and in the Church, by contrast to political parties, those opposed to change can easily find 'ideological' (i.e. theological) grounds for opposing it.

We have expressed the tensions between unchanging principles/beliefs and their contemporary application in terms of the opposition between 'church' and 'world', and we have used traditional theological language to describe the dilemma faced by both churches and political parties. This distinction is, however, abstract since any church is part of the world. Both church and world are equally fallen; the church is that part of the fallen world which has been redeemed. Equally, the distinction between church and society is abstract, since concretely any church is part of society and thereby subject to change just as society is. If, however, these pairs of terms are seen as referring to distinct entities, the distinction becomes that between two social groups, one concerned with unchanging religious matters and the other with temporal/secular (i.e. changing) states of affairs. As a result, the religious becomes associated with the unchanging, and the secular with the changing, and any change in a church is seen as an abandonment of its unchanging religious character. These confusions would seem to lie behind the divisions among the laity on the issue of change in the Church, one of the two dimensions on which, as noted in Chapter 7, the laity are most divided. However, when asked directly about their attitudes towards the world only two-fifths of responding laity regarded it in a negative way, while over 90 per cent saw it as the object of evangelism, and a similarly large majority saw it as the object of loving service on the part of the Church. These 'world-accepting' attitudes are what one would expect from a post-established *ecclesia* rather than an exclusive sect. The lack of relation between such attitudes and their approach to change in the Church suggests, however, that the laity have not considered the relationship between changes in traditional Church practice and organization, and the fulfilment of its mission towards the 'world' in the sense of that part of society which lies outside the Church.

The most striking example of the difficulties facing the Church in a postmodern society is that concerning sexual morality. A simplistic church/world distinction would line up morality on the side of the Church, and immorality and depravity on that of the world, and see the mission of the Church as saving individuals from the world by instilling traditional standards of sexual morality into them. While we may assume immorality and depravity to be universal features of social life, they tend to be characteristic of only a minority of any population. What the churches face today is a situation where there exists a number of different standards of morality, of which the Christian is only one. What baffles the traditional Christian is that deviations from traditional Christian standards are pursued conscientiously and that those standards are regarded negatively from the moral standpoints of people practising such deviations. Once again, there has been a collapse of a traditional hegemony, this time of traditional Christian morality in the sexual sphere, without its replacement by any identifiable alternative. If the Church decided to throw tradition to the winds, to sell out its traditional moral principles and conform to those of the world, it would be faced with a choice between a bewildering variety of alternatives. And this, indeed, is one of the defining characteristics of postmodernity: namely, the replacement of a single dominant standard by a number of alternative standards, intellectual and aesthetic as well as moral. Across the postmodern landscape – to be likened to a market made up of a whole set of stalls, each peddling its own set of standards, between which the conscientious individual has to make a personal choice – there blows a mighty rushing wind. This wind is that not of the Holy Spirit but of the spirit of the age (or more accurately of the decade), which is the result of people's attempts to make sense of their diverse and ever-changing cultural experience, which finds its most marked expression among the young. The parishes recognized this phenomenon and were quite clear that, whether they favoured change in the Church or not, these ever-changing currents were the new things that St Paul urged the Church not to rush after.

9

The Church in a time of rapid social change

The previous chapter has suggested that the Church in Wales should not, in order to survive, attempt to embark on wholesale organizational and doctrinal change in the fashion of New Labour. On the contrary, it may well be that the most valuable contribution that the Church in Wales can make in a postmodern society is to provide a solid alternative to the flimsy and evanescent moral fashions of postmodern culture. Its solidity derives from the fact that it is not peddling detailed prescriptions about how to behave appropriate to a stable and less differentiated society but that, in common with the other Christian Churches and, indeed, other world religions, its attempts to find ways through the perplexities thrown up by contemporary society are rooted in a coherent 'world view' of the nature of humankind and its spiritual, social and material needs – a world view which is 'not of an age but for all time'. That said, it will be of little use to the Church or the world if that view is set out, Sunday by Sunday, by overworked clergy in dimly lit, ill-kept churches, to a dwindling band of old-age pensioners singing from Hymns Ancient and Mid-Victorian. This, it must be emphasized, is emphatically not a description of the Church in Wales as it faces the new millennium. On the contrary, the Church is reasonably well placed in terms of resources to face the challenges of the coming decades, and our conclusions concerning the devotion of both clergy and the active laity have been generally upbeat. But it is *one* of many possible futures for the Church, and one that becomes increasingly probable the greater the extent to which those challenges are ducked and not faced. Facing them, however, is going to require some degree of change.

The evidence of this study serves to identify important factors which affect the ability of the Church to innovate or reform, at a time when changes in the wider society appear to set new priorities. Manifestly, where members are divided on the need for change, innovation becomes problematical. However, this raises directly the question as to why they are divided, which itself points to the deeper issue of justifying change within an institution where legitimation derives primarily from theology and Church tradition. Where the terms in which the faith is couched are wearing out, and the faithful are struggling therefore to express it in new terms, the previous grasp of the faith is weakened and the intellectual demands made on believers are increased. A significant minority of the laity appears to be in this position, while the majority seems to be reasonably happy with traditional formulations. This means that those with a secure grasp of the faith see no need to express it in new terms, while those most open to change lack the ability to make informed judgements concerning the validity or otherwise of any such changes as might be proposed.

There are also major problems concerned with the direction of any change. The attraction of the Christian religion, from its very beginnings, was its distinctive character within the social world in which it was set. The language of Jesus' teaching and early Christian writings was, however, very much of its age and accessible to those to whom it was directed. There is a danger in confusing the message and the language in which it is couched. In the attempt to communicate the message, it is vital that its distinctiveness is not lost, and an essentially religious message is not secularized. That message is premised on a world view which asserts the existence of a spiritual reality, lying beyond the empirical appearance of things, which broke through into the material world uniquely in Jesus Christ. This world view is fundamentally opposed to the intellectual fashion called 'postmodernism', which threatens to deny the distinction between appearance and reality, the sign and the thing signified; between it and the Christian Gospel there can be no accommodation. On the other hand, to say that the Church is set in a secular society is to imply that the culture of that society is such that religious ideas can be dismissed as 'unscientific beliefs in the supernatural'. What must not be lost sight of is that to say that our culture is postmodern is to assert that not only has the religious world view lost its hegemony but so has its rival for hegemony – namely, secular humanism. The postmodern world is one where no world view is hegemonic, and it would be fatal to suppose that in the doctrinal and pedagogic sphere change must involve doing some sort of deal with secular humanism. It is not only generals that fight the last war instead of this one. The arrival of the chaotic pluralism of postmodern culture, like the end of the Cold War, provides an opportunity for the positive assertion of the validity of belief systems rather than their defence on grounds chosen by their principal opponents. The barrier to this change is the relatively elderly character of both clergy and people, whose mind-sets were cast in an earlier intellectual age.

Innovation may be made more difficult because of limitations of an organizational or political kind – for instance, by the existence of an elaborate system of ecclesiastical units designed to maintain terrritorial coverage, or the fact that the Church is a 'grouping' of dioceses rather than an entity substantially directed from the centre. Indeed, the effects of these types of factor can ramify: as has been shown, administrative and resource issues have led to the clergy re-emphasizing traditional aspects of their role which make it inimical to reinterpretation – a position which has been accepted by the laity, both parties being comfortable with a set of role definitions based on an inappropriate use of the sacred/profane distinction. Moreover, the continued reduction of central financial support, and hence the greater emphasis on giving at the parochial level, is likely to reinforce the conception of the Church as a fellowship of local churches, with the result that the prime purpose of individual giving comes to be seen as payment for the provision of local facilities. Indeed, this is already the case; covenanted giving usually flows into the coffers of the local church, not into those of the Representative Body; the whole thrust of contemporary stewardship campaigns is to make members willing to shoulder the responsibility for the payment of 'their' clergy. Hence the attempt to introduce change through the promotion of Christian Stewardship is likely to inhibit change at the bottom of an organization where, as at the top, the emphasis is on the preservation of each local church at all costs rather than on increasing the funds available to further the mission of the Church in the Province as a whole.

Given that the Christian faith may be expressed in different ways, then in this study we are concerned with the Welsh institutional embodiment of its Anglican expression. The survival of the Church in Wales depends on its maintaining an expression of the Christian faith which is distinctively both Welsh and Anglican. This raises an even more serious problem as regards change. In so far as the difference between the Christian Churches consists in their mode of expression of the one faith, and modes of expression of a religious faith need to change as the culture of the society in which they exist changes, how in the face of massive cultural change can any given denomination survive as a distinct entity within the Christian Church? It is certainly the case that, in a typically postmodern way, Christian denominations no longer claim to have a monopoly of Christian truth, and differences between them have become matters of style, presentation, religious atmosphere and tradition – have, in a word, become cultural rather than doctrinal differences. It follows that changes in the way the faith is expressed within the Church in Wales may be opposed not on theological grounds but on the grounds that it involves a break with Anglican tradition. Moreover, because it is loyalty to that tradition that keeps the faithful within the Anglican Church, and through it within the Christian Church as a whole, changes in the expression (doctrinal formulation, worship, fellowship) of the Christian faith within the Anglican Church may result in its desertion by its most faithful members.

Few people live in the heaven of general ideas. However clearly they grasp the principles of their belief, however passionately they hold them and however conscientiously they follow them, they do so under particular cultural, social and material circumstances. As a result, the particular comes to signify the general, and the general the particular. It is through the local church with its own buildings, its fellowship of particular individuals, its particular forms of preaching and worship that the Gospel is received. It is through a particular language and translation that they hear the message of the Bible. To be manifest, the general has to be incarnate in the particular and so becomes identified with it. Equally the particular – in the sense of the person and his or her religious and emotional experiences – becomes identified with the settings of its occurrence. The sign becomes identical with the thing signified. It is this fact rather than any devotion to tradition as such that makes it so hard to close a church, amalgamate benefices, state doctrines in different terms or revise the liturgy, and that makes the sanctification of the particular a universal religious phenomenon. Historically, however, the charge brought against the Church in Wales as a branch of the *Anglican* Communion is, as we saw in Chapter 1, that it has been insufficiently identified with the particular society of which it is part. It is appropriate, therefore, to consider briefly the nature of the Church as a Welsh institution.

The Church as a Welsh institution

The Church in Wales may be characterized as a major Welsh national, territorial and public institution, it being 'national' in the sense that its system of territorial units essentially covers the Principality, it being 'public' in that it offers its services to all. Importantly, despite some reduction in clergy numbers and some grouping of parishes, the Church has been able to maintain the traditional parochial system. As well as maintaining full territorial coverage, it evidently expends considerable effort in responding to local differences and needs – for example, in terms of rural/urban differences and in respect of language. Although the Church is disestablished, and despite secularization, the commitment to Anglicanism in Wales is broadly of the same order as that in England.

In considering the question of Welshness further, one can usefully distinguish institutional and cultural aspects. At the institutional level the Church speaks for Wales in two contexts, ecclesiastical and secular. Through its archbishops and bishops it represents Wales at the decennial conference of Anglican bishops from across the world (the Lambeth Conference). Through the Anglican Consultative Council (ACC), the 'standing committee' of the Anglican Communion, international contacts are continuous with, for instance, the Church in Wales hosting a meeting of the ACC in Cardiff in 1990. The Lambeth Conferences are also supplemented by more frequent meetings of the primates of the Communion at which Wales is represented by its archbishop.

To the claim that the Church represents Wales internationally, it may be objected that what is represented is not Wales but the Church in Wales. However, this objection is, arguably, rebutted once account is taken of the extent to which the Church as an institution represents Wales in secular contexts. We shall describe below how in recent decades the Church, either alone or with other bodies, has been highly active in such spheres as education and social policy, generating reports on a large number of Welsh social issues. Hence, the Church has in the last thirty years provided a major input into the discussion of distinctively Welsh problems and issues. This increasing activity in the secular sphere is partly a result of its representative function in the ecclesiastical sphere, since that function continually requires it to relate wider issues to Wales, to report the way in which they affect Wales and to make a distinctively Welsh contribution to Anglican discussions of them. In both spheres the Church has come to represent Wales in the sense that the views it puts forward concern issues of contemporary relevance to all the people of Wales and do not merely concern narrowly religious matters.

Turning to the issue of whether the Church is culturally, including linguistically, representative of Wales, it is worth initially noting that the debates of the Church's Governing Body are conducted in both languages (with simultaneous translation for English monoglots). For the last twenty years non-Welsh-speaking bishops have been the exception rather than the rule, and three of the four most recent archbishops have had Welsh as their first language. Language is not, however, the only cultural marker. For instance, one can consider the contents of one of the Church's own journals, *Theologica Cambrensis* (now *Theology Wales*), founded in 1988. Narrowly theological contributions have recently formed only about one-third of its contents; in the remaining space, articles on broadly social issues are interspersed with contributions directed at specifically Welsh concerns; indeed, recent issues have seen some fusion of these two streams.

In turning to our survey evidence, attention may be directed at the similarity of two figures. Benefices whose services were conducted at least partly in Welsh constituted 37 per cent, while 34 per cent of incumbents were able to preach in Welsh. When compared with the overall percentage of Welsh speakers in the Principality these figures appear satisfactory, although it can be shown that there is a certain bias towards monoglot English services in urban areas, which reduces the effectiveness of the Church in ministering to urban Welsh speakers (Harris and Startup 1995, 109). However, in respect of the clergy, it could conceivably have been the case that, Welsh speakers apart, they comprised chiefly English expatriates. In fact, only 7 per cent had been ordained outside Wales and the amount of movement to the Church in Wales from the Church of England was small, with only 13 per cent having served in dioceses outside Wales. In Chapters 1 and 7 we have also shown that, as far as the laity of the Church in Wales is concerned, it is in no sense the 'Church of the English' in Wales.

In sum, the Church in Wales is a major national Welsh institution, substantially resourced and geographically extensive, which ought to be able to exercise a pervasive influence on Welsh life. It is, however, the perception of both its leaders and outsiders that, although there is no lack of 'Welshness', it tends to be less influential than its size and extent suggest. There appear to be two main reasons for this. Among the laity the elderly, the retired and women are over-represented, and this must seriously limit the Church's effectiveness. The second point is that, as we have seen, given the imperative to maintain an inclusive territorial structure, members tend to concentrate on 'survival', which turns them inwards rather than outwards.

Provincial activities and responses

In considering the future of the Church in Wales, it is vital to make some mention of the activities of the Church at the provincial level and to note some of the major changes that have taken place in those activities most directly relevant since the present study was initiated. The focus of attention here must be the work of the Board of Mission, which in 1990 had six 'divisions': Education; Communication; Ecumenism and World Mission; Social Responsibility; Evangelism and Adult Education; and Stewardship. In the mid-nineties, World Mission became a separate division, Adult Education became part of Education, and, most significantly, Evangelism was replaced by 'Parish Development and Renewal'. The creation of this new division signalled an important shift in emphasis in the work of the board.

The activities listed were first grouped together under the aegis of the board in the mid-eighties. Since then, the board has been concerned both with studies and reports and with action on those reports. However, the recommendations that ensued were necessarily made at the provincial level, though the action called for was often required of dioceses and parishes. One of the most prolific producers of reports was the division for Social Responsibility. During the eighties its predecessor produced a series of reports on topics of current social concern: racism, euthanasia, the future of work, genetic engineering, housing and homelessness, human and animal rights. The division continued in this tradition: it responded to the report of the Church of England's commission on Urban Priority Areas, *Faith in the City* (1985), with a three-part report *Faith in Wales* (1989–91), which included a picture of socio-economic conditions throughout Wales. Again, the Church of England's report *Faith in the Countryside* (1990) was followed by a splendid report entitled *The Church in the Welsh Countryside: A Programme for Action for the Church in Wales* (1992). During the nineties it has dealt, in one form or another, with the following topics: bio-ethics, sexuality, community development, housing, poverty, the 'Poll Tax', women, children, the Lottery, Welsh Language Legislation, changes in local government, and the role of the Church in 'disaster' situations. Moreover, most of the topics listed (which do not reflect the work of the International Sector of the division) have been dealt with in British national and European, as well as in Welsh national, contexts, and often with an ecumenical dimension. When taken together with the outputs of the other divisions of the Board, the range of activities and the quality of the work done are impressive and, indeed, remarkable for a relatively small Church of a country that is 'peripheral' in both British and European terms. An adequate account of them over the last twenty years would require at least a chapter. If the activities of all the other provincial bodies, such as, for example, the Liturgical Commission (which has responded to dissatisfactions with the existing liturgy by issuing a new alternative form of service in 1994) were to be included, an adequate account would probably be the length of a short book. Through its activities at the provincial level the Church in Wales makes an important contribution to public life at both the Welsh and the British national levels, to the Anglican Communion and to the worldwide Church. *Inevitably*, much of this activity goes 'over the head' (in one sense or another) of most of the laity – and probably many of the clergy – in the parishes.

One of the characteristics of 'postmodern' society is held to be that it is in the process of 'globalization'. This does not mean simply that the different territorial groups into which the world's population is divided constitute the conditions of each other's action. It implies, rather, the existence of global processes which interpenetrate and directly affect the lives of even the smallest territorial groups. In Giddens's words, 'Globalization ... is not just ... to do with very large-scale influences. It is also an "in here" phenomenon, directly bound up with the circumstances of local life' (1994, 80–1). It was one of the strengths of the report on the *The Church in the Welsh Countryside* that it implicitly recognized this fact and dealt with issues such as housing, in-migration, poverty and unemployment as integral to the daily lives of the inhabitants of Welsh rural communities, and not as events taking place at some high, 'macro' level. Though the discussions of major social problems at the provincial level are inevitably over the heads of most of the laity in the parishes, the reality they discuss is to be found locally and is not merely a property of populations represented by the political institutions of Cardiff, Westminster, Brussels and the UN. That said, of the fifty-three specific recommendations of *The Church in the Welsh Countryside*, thirty specify action at the provincial level, three ecumenical action, thirteen action at the diocesan level, but only seven action at the parish level. Now many of these, if acted upon by the bodies to whom they were directed, would have had major implications for parishes. However, recommendations that parishes should do this, that or the other figured low in the report because its authors knew that their proposals would have had little effect since parishes lacked the competence to carry them out – by themselves. The report naturally concentrated its recommendations on the diocesan and provincial levels: that is to say, upon bodies with the capacity to effect them.

The report of the preliminary survey of the State of the Church Study (Harris 1990a) concluded with the heartfelt plea of one incumbent, on the topic of evangelism, as follows:

If I were able to ask for anything to come out of this enquiry and its subsequent developments it would be that we end up with people and not paper. What I have in mind is people, be they Diocesan Missioners ... or whatever, who will come out into ... the parishes to encourage,

guide, help and empower us, both clergy and laity, and push us down
... the essential road of evangelism. This would not be, I hasten to
add, a case of 'them' doing it for or to us, but a true partnership of
using and sharing the gifts for the sake of the Kingdom.

What this respondent was enunciating was one of the cardinal
principles of 'community development'. Community development is something in which the Church in Wales has been
involved for the last ten years (1986–96), in partnership with the
Children's Society. This partnership has involved programmes of
community development in the Welsh dioceses and has recently
been extended. A key value which underpins practice is 'working
with rather than *for* people and being accountable to them'
(Church in Wales: Board of Mission 1993, 33).

Having learned this lesson, the Church has begun to apply it in
the creation, in 1995, of the division for Parish Development and
Renewal. The formation of the division was inspired by the use of
a method employed on the Roman Catholic archdiocese of
Dublin whereby 'the members of the division are involved in
dioceses and parishes and their experience forms part of the division's on-going research' (Church in Wales: Board of Mission
1997, 10). In addition, the Board has embarked on a programme
of 'encouragement projects' operating at the deanery level. All
these moves supplement earlier initiatives which were designed to
empower the parishes for evangelism, such as the appointment of
a peripatetic 'trainer in evangelism' during the first three years of
the decade, the compilation of a directory of resource people, and
the creation of a resource publication containing articles on
mission, renewal and evangelism.

While all these changes and developments witness to the
energy and vitality of the Church in Wales, it is possible to question how adequate they can be to reorient the majority of parishes
and their clergy 'from maintenance to mission'. Encouragement
projects will affect one deanery (out of seventy-seven) a year in
the last five years of the decade. Given what we have said about
the present clergy–laity relationship, the key to their success is, as
always, the enthusiasm and support of the clergy. In this regard
it is important to note that the clergy load is slowly but steadily
increasing. As a result of grouping, the number of benefices has
declined from 604 at the time of the preliminary survey in

January 1989 to 583 on 31 December 1996. The figures describing the annual inflow and outflow of full-time parochial clergy over the same period show an average annual loss of approximately three (Church in Wales: Reports of the Board of Ministry, 1990–7). It is likely that clergy numbers will continue to decline in the next ten years, unless there is a substantial increase in the number of ordinands. However, were the numbers of stipendiary clergy to rise there would have to be a corresponding increase in the diocesan quotas to pay for them, which would impose a further money-raising burden on the parishes and their clergy. In these circumstances of increasing burdens upon the parochial clergy, any enthusiasm for parish development is likely to be dampened by their preoccupation with more immediate concerns. These factors necessarily militate against the efforts by the centre to effect change at the parochial level.

To recognize such factors is not to dismiss the strategy of the Board of Mission in the matter of evangelism as impractical but merely to draw attention to the limitations which the present state of the Church inevitably imposes upon the success of such a strategy. The hope must be that one of its immediate effects will be the training of future trainers so that the personnel available for 'encouragement' and 'development' increases geometrically. Even if this were to happen, however, the Decade of Evangelism would be no more than a first step in a long-term process which would probably have little effect on the declining numbers of adherents until well into the twenty-first century.

Growth or decline?

Having noted the character and implications of some of our data, we can review the present position and prospects for the Church in Wales in the light of theory within the sociology of religion. In the literature many factors in church growth have been suggested (Hoge 1979; Finke and Stark 1992), but it may be valuable in the present context initially to situate the discussion with respect to the factor of 'strictness', highlighted in the American literature, in order to draw out some important differences between movements and churches, both liberal and conservative.

Kelley (1977) presents a view of an ideal type of religion within which strictness is a necessary condition of organizational strength. The making of demands on members ensures they will be committed, while also serving as a sign to others of a serious church. He explains the decline of the Roman Catholic Church following the Second Vatican Council by reference to the relaxation of demanding rules which might be taken as a signal that the Church was no longer serious about religion. Kelley specifically asserts: 'The quality which makes one system of ultimate meaning more convincing is not its content but its seriousness/costliness/strictness' (Kelley 1977, 170). The issue of the importance of content is taken up below, but there is no denying that considerations of strictness are relevant to a church's prospects. In this connection Iannaccone (1994) presents a modified version of Kelley's argument; and in some associated work a useful framework for analysing the potential for the growth or decline of religious movements is beginning to be established (Stark 1996). The strength of that argument has recently been demonstrated through a consideration of the growth of the Jehovah's Witnesses (Stark and Iannaccone 1997). It is worth noting some of the key propositions of the framework.

It is claimed that religious movements are likely to succeed to the extent that they maintain a medium level of tension with their surrounding environment – are strict but not too strict, where strictness refers to the maintenance of a distinctive lifestyle or morality in personal and family life (Iannaccone 1994, 1190). In addition, it is asserted that as the 'costs' of membership rise, so the net gains of membership increase too from higher levels of the production of collective goods. Obviously, in order to succeed a movement requires legitimate leaders with adequate authority. However, it is noted that success seems to be associated with the absence of the usual model of authority based on a distinction between clergy and laity. A further notion is that religious movements must maintain a level of fertility sufficient to offset member mortality, and that continuing growth depends upon not only bringing people in but letting go of those who do not fit in. It follows, therefore, that successful movements must socialize the young sufficiently well to minimize both defection and the appeal of reduced strictness.

While this framework of propositions was explicitly developed in relation to movements, when considered in relation to the Church in Wales it has the value of highlighting issues and problem areas for the future which are suggestive of continuing decline. That Church is at the lower end of the continuum in respect of strictness in two senses. Given inclusivity, there are many individuals acknowledged as 'members' who are minimally active (or even inactive). However, as important, even among the active 'faithful' (as has been shown), there is evidence of widely diverse (including incompatible) views. The Church is indeed notably 'strict' in its traditional toleration of this diversity. While the 'costs' of membership tend to be low, so too are the net gains from membership: for instance, the experience of a service will tend to be diminished when the church is more than half empty. A further problem is that most participants conspire in the preservation of a conventional hierarchical distinction between clergy and laity. Clergy attitudes fail to promote a sharing of the whole ministry of the Church, both pastoral and evangelistic, between clergy and laity; on the other hand, many of the laity identify the clergy with the Church. In addition the demographics of the Church could hardly look less promising: there must be real doubts whether the population of active members is replacing itself. Young adults are poorly represented among the active laity, and there is no emphasis on providing important roles for them. Even to moderate its decline, the Church seems implicitly reliant on the validity of the idea that there is drift back towards religion in old age.

Having noted some implications of strictness, let us return to the issue of whether 'content' is indeed as relatively unimportant as Kelley (1977) suggests. Prima-facie doubts on this score are not diminished by consideration of the parallel with politics. In the democracies, just how successful are highly disciplined political parties of the Left and Right compared with the relatively non-ideological and traditionally moderate Left, Centre and Right groupings – themselves often significantly characterized as 'broad churches'? All evidence suggests that the 'stricter' political groups are generally relatively unsuccessful and often ephemeral. To this point it may be objected that politics, unlike religion, is 'this-worldly' and centrally concerned with notions which may be evaluated through practical experience. The ideas of extreme Left or extreme Right groups, for instance, may be rejected given political experience here or elsewhere. By contrast, the claims of religious groups about (say) the afterlife are not similarly subject to practical/experiential test. While this points up a key difference, it is nevertheless quite wrong to conclude that religious 'content' substantially lacks implications which bear upon recruitment or retention of members – for example, the Catholic Church may have difficulty recruiting priests while requiring them to be male and celibate; that Church may likewise fail to retain members whose experience leads them to be critical of its stand on birth control. Again, in the Anglican community, divorced former members may drift away where they are unable to remarry in church.

More generally, against Kelley's virtually 'timeless' approach, it may be suggested that specific 'content' can be very important for growth or decline either through its relation with a cultural or religious tradition or through its accommodation of, or failure to accommodate, modern concepts. On the first point, it is apparent that those brought up within a Christian tradition are only exceptionally converted directly to a wholly non-Christian religion, whatever its position on the strictness dimension; the predominant pattern is that conversion is towards a set of ideas which is meaningful in the light of one's spiritual starting-point. On the second point, Tamney and Johnson (1998; see also Tamney 1992) have drawn attention to some values associated with modernity, such as individualism and anti-dogmatism, and affirm: 'Strictness, as defined by Kelley, is inconsistent with independence, cosmopolitanism, and accepting doubt' (1998, 211). These authors proceed to claim that as people are exposed to such modernizing processes as formal education, it is to be expected that they will be less attracted to strict Churches. Nor need the relevant conceptions be confined to values: the compatibility of religious 'content' with established scientific and technological notions and explanations is also potentially relevant. In this connection the Church in Wales may be characterized as a mainline church in the Christian tradition which has strained towards the accommodation of modern values – for example, in relation to equality of the sexes (as evidenced by the ordination of women) and to family planning; nor is it conscious of any conflict between its ideas and those of modern science and technology. No doubt associated with this, its congregation is disproportionately middle class and above average in terms of years of formal education.

The above analysis should help to clarify a key point, which Kelley's overemphasis on strictness threatens to obscure. To return to the above example concerning the relaxation of certain rules following the Second Vatican Council: the associated problem for the Roman Catholic Church did not hinge primarily on declining strictness as such but, rather, on the issue of legitimation – that is, on how to justify the change. This will always be a problem for any institution within which the fundamental basis of legitimation is by reference to Scripture or church tradition. Indeed, the key problem for mainline churches in the modern era is precisely the tension between the dictates of tradition and of modern values. To take an example: few would contest that the ordination of women forms part of a modern feminist 'agenda'; what is altogether less clear is how this innovation flows from a reading of the Bible or an understanding of Church tradition. Indeed, similar tension in respect of the position of gay priests and homosexual activity threatens to divide the Anglican community at the present time. A church which travels too far with modernity threatens its own basis of legitimation. While mainline denominations are struggling with issues of this kind, it is wholly unsurprising that conservative Protestant sects can make headway with a reassertion of Scripture, particularly among sections of the population less imbued with characteristically modern values.

An implication of the above discussion concerns the interplay between the two elements of 'strictness' and 'content'. If a church is to be strict, what should it be strict about? This issue arose for the early Christians in relation to the practice of circumcision; a not unimportant issue of the moment concerns the view to be taken of homosexual activity. However, without being facile, from the point of view of a liberal church the key point is that responsible, caring, orderly and spiritually meaningful lives may be led both by circumcised and non-circumcised individuals, and both by practising and non-practising homosexuals (which is not to say, in respect of the latter, that objection may not properly be taken to high levels of promiscuity or to such practices as cottaging). 'Strictness' in respect of lifestyle or morality in personal and domestic life implies adherence to principles but need not involve rigid conformity to rules in either of these identified respects. Principles rather than narrow rules are at the heart of the distinction between conservative and liberal Christianity. That being understood, an area where there does appear to be a real need for greater 'strictness' by the Church concerns the grasp by members of the nature of the Church as a divine institution (see particularly Chapter 6) – that is to say, more education is needed in the essentials of the faith. As part of this, there needs to be an understanding of the right relationship between the roles of clergy and of laity, this being simultaneously of both doctrinal and great practical importance. More generally, the relation between theology and various practicalities needs to be thought through and acted upon, and this will involve confronting both resource and organizational issues. To illustrate: greater understanding is needed of the notion that Christians are called to the stewardship of God's gifts but, among other things, this should lead directly on to greater adherence to realistic guidelines in respect of responsible personal giving. In this way a better grasp of theology may invigorate the Church.

The Church within a religious economy

An important point to make about Stark's (1996) framework for analysing the potential of religious movements (considered above) is that his various propositions imply the limits to growth encountered by *sects* as much as they delineate its necessary preconditions. Indeed, historical studies of Christianity in Britain and elsewhere tend to suggest that periodic 'revivals' are necessary to the maintenance of the membership of religious groups in societies where some degree of secularization has taken place (Cragg 1960; Stark and Bainbridge 1985; Gill 1993). Such revivals usually require their adherents to conform to relatively strict standards of behaviour which, while the basis of the sect's appeal, necessarily limit its range. In the past this was associated with upward economic mobility, which limited the social range of the appeal and also resulted in lower fertility. As a result the sect becomes less strict, more inclusive and more respectable – becomes, in fact, a denomination rather than a sect. Unable to reproduce itself biologically and having lost its capacity to recruit new members and retain its youth, it inevitably declines unless a 'revival' restores some of its sect-like qualities. Now, while these considerations apply to a sect, they do not apply to an inclusive church as a whole; rather, they apply to religious movements within it, which are the means of its renewal. The Church in Wales is a post-establishment church within a secular society with a postmodern culture. Such a church must have some of the characteristic qualities of a denomination and therefore be subject to the same processes of decline.

In the first place, there is a trade-off between two aspects of the level of demands made on members. A high level of demands establishes a difference between members and non-members and is therefore attractive (membership means something), but if the level is too high membership will be rejected as too costly. It seems likely that, in the Church in Wales, while the contribution made by the active faithful is very high, the level of demands made upon the general membership is too low: being an active member of St X's is therefore highly meaningful both to the active and to those outside the Church, but being an Anglican as such has come to mean very little.

Secondly, and relatedly, this study has argued that, while the orthodox theological conception of the relation between clergy and laity in the Anglican tradition is of a kind which is likely to be highly conducive to the creation of strong and attractive local religious groups, in practice and at the level of consciousness this conception is widely misunderstood.

Thirdly, the age structure of the membership of the Church is such that decline in membership would be inevitable, even if there was no decline in *rates* of attendance of members or loss of members or members' children – unless, of course, demographic losses were replaced by new converts. However, there is loss of both members and members' children. A recent study (Richter and Francis 1998) of church-leavers in Britain has again drawn attention to the failure of the Church to keep in touch with baptized persons (or their parents) and confirmands and urge them to participate. Commenting on the report in the *Observer* (21 December 1997), Sir John Harvey Jones made the extremely practical point that 'it costs six times as much to win new customers as it does to keep the ones you have got'. The failure of mainstream Churches, including the Church in Wales, to increase their active membership by exploiting the opportunities offered by the existence of a large reservoir of inactive members is quite extraordinary.

The ability to attract adherents has not depended, historically, simply on the characteristics of the faith and religious practice of a religious group. The membership of such groups in a society that was plural in the religious sense has always had a social significance: to be a member of one group was to define oneself as a non-member of another group, as the terms 'Nonconformist' and 'Dissenter' imply. Historians (e.g. Hastings 1991) have argued that the decline in Nonconformity in the twentieth century is closely connected with its success in achieving its political aims at the end of the nineteenth, and in Wales these included the disestablishment of the Welsh part of the Anglican Church as well as the removal of disabilities which had more generally been placed on Dissenters. Conversely, to be Anglican was to be not a Nonconformist. This social meaning of Anglican membership has lost its salience, so that, in so far as the attractiveness of the Anglican faith depends on its difference, that difference has to be religious; the significance of Anglican membership as a sign of erstwhile social-group membership has all but evaporated.

So far the argument of these two concluding chapters has been that the survival of the Church in Wales depends upon its ability to adapt to the fundamental changes taking place in society and culture in the late twentieth century and that this adaptation involves major change. It should by now be clear that adaptation does not imply the creation of a 'new' Church in Wales on the lines of the 'new' Labour Party. Indeed, it requires in some instances, such as the recovery of the idea of the Church as the *laos*, a return to tradition rather than its abandonment. But it does require the recognition that what might be called the 'religious economy' has changed out of all recognition.

One can talk of a religious economy, since the word 'economy' derives from the Greek *oikos* or 'household'. The Church in Wales belongs to the 'household of faith', and it is for this reason that the term given to attempts to heal the divisions between different Christian Churches is 'ecumenical', expressing a concern for the whole household. The term 'household' originally referred to a self-subsistent group whose autonomous nature was the result of the different activities of its members. The relevance of this concept to the Church in Wales, living as it does as part of a secular society characterized by religious pluralism and having a postmodern culture, is twofold.

Instead of thinking of *the* relationship between a church and society, it is necessary to see the connection between the two as made up of sets of different types of relationship which vary between parishes, benefices, deaneries and dioceses. There is no way in which 'the Church' at the provincial level can respond simultaneously to all these types of relationship. The response of the Church as a province will comprise, rather, the responses of the different members of the Anglican household of faith in Wales. The same is true at the parochial level: neither individual members nor any single parochial activity can itself satisfy the demands made by those relationships at the same time. Each parish needs to produce a variety of responses instead of seeking the will-o'-the-wisp of the 'right' response.

The Church in Wales is, however, only one member of the wider Christian household in Wales. A recent study (Chambers 2000) suggests that the Welsh household of faith is an economy in a more modern sense, in that there is an exchange of adherents between different denominations and individual churches, each satisfying the religious needs of different age groups and social classes. One of the things that is required of the Church in Wales is that it reforge its Anglican identity by defining what is its distinctive role in this religious economy. That identity is defined sociologically by its being an *ecclesia*. *Ecclesiae* are inclusive. Inclusivity does not, however, refer only to social inclusivity; it has also referred historically to the inclusion of different types and forms of religious witness and service. Because other relationships are being dealt with by Churches of other denominations in the area, a parish may focus on a particular relation with society into which to enter to witness to the Gospel. An inclusive Church will include all these types of relationship. The Church as a province will avoid the specialization which necessarily characterizes particular denominations and local churches. The various ministries at every level of the Church need, however, to be brought into relation, and each needs to be enriched and corrected by the understandings yielded by the others. It is this function that the Church in Wales, by virtue of both its order and its organization, is uniquely placed to serve.

References

ACORA (Archbishop's Commission on Rural Areas) (1990). *Faith in the Countryside* (Worthing, Churchman).

Aldridge, A. (1987). 'In the absence of the minister: structures of subordination in the role of deaconess in the Church of England', *Sociology*, 21:3, 377–92.

—— (1989). 'Men, women and clergymen: opinion and authority in a sacred organisation', *Sociological Review*, 37:1, 43–64.

—— (1992). 'Discourse on women in the clerical profession', *Sociology*, 26:1, 45–57.

Argyle, M. (1958). *Religious Behaviour* (London, Routledge & Kegan Paul).

Bellah, R. N. (1957). *Tokugawa Religion* (New York, Free Press).

—— (1970). *Beyond Belief* (New York, Harper & Row).

Beveridge, W. E. (1971). *Managing the Church* (London, SCM).

Blizzard, S. W. (1956). 'The minister's dilemma', *Christian Century*, 73, 508–9.

—— (1985). *The Protestant Parish Minister: A Behavioral Science Interpretation* (Storrs, Conn., Society for the Scientific Study of Religion).

Brierley, P. (1983). *Prospects for Wales from a Census of the Churches in 1982* (London, MARC Europe/Bible Society).

—— (1985). *A Century of British Christianity* (London, MARC Europe/Bible Society).

—— (ed.) (1991). *Prospects for the Nineties* (London, MARC Europe).

Brierley, P. and Evans, B. (1983). *Yr Argoelion yn Adroddiad o Gyfrifiad yr Eglwysi* (London, MARC Europe/Cymdeithas y Beibl).

Brierley, P. and Hiscock, V. (eds.) (1993). *UK Christian Handbook* (London, Christian Research Association).

Bruce, S. (1995a). *Religion in Modern Britain* (Oxford, Oxford University Press).

—— (1995b). *Religion and Modernization* (Oxford, Oxford University Press).

Chadwick, O. (1990). *The Secularization of the European Mind in the Nineteenth Century* (Cambridge, Canto). (First published Cambridge, Cambridge University Press, 1975.)

Chambers, P. R. (2000). 'Church Growth and Decline in Swansea' (Unpub. Ph.D. thesis, University of Wales).

Church in Wales: Commission on the Boundaries and Structure of the Church in Wales (1974). *Second Interim Report* (Cardiff, Governing Body of the Church in Wales).

—— (1978). *Final Report* (Cardiff, Governing Body of the Church in Wales).

Church in Wales: Board of Ministry (1990–7). *Annual Reports* (Cardiff, Governing Body of the Church in Wales).

Church in Wales: Board of Mission (1993). *Annual Report 1992* (Penarth, Church in Wales Publications).

—— (1997). *Annual Review 1996* (Penarth, Church in Wales Publications).

Church in Wales: Board of Mission: Division for Social Responsibility (1989–91). *Faith in Wales* (Penarth, Church in Wales Publications).

—— (1992) *The Church in the Welsh Countryside: A Programme of Action for the Church in Wales* (Penarth, Church in Wales Publications).

Church in Wales Governing Body (1992–7). *Membership and Finances: 1990–91 to 1995–6* (Cardiff, Governing Body of the Church in Wales).

Church of England: Advisory Council for the Church's Ministry (1971). *Bishops and Dioceses* (London, Church Information Office).

Church of England: Central Board of Finance (1997). *Church Statistics* (London).

Church of England: Commission on Urban Priority Areas (1985). *Faith in the City* (London, Church House Publishing).

Church of England: Commission on Rural Areas (1990). *Faith in the Countryside* (London, Church House Publishing).

Commission on Social Justice (1994). *Social Justice: Strategies for National Renewal* (London, Vintage).

Cragg, G. R. (1960). *The Church in the Age of Reason* (London, Hodder & Stoughton).

Davie, G. (1994). *Religion in Britain since 1945* (Oxford, Blackwell).

Davies, D., Pack, C., Seymour, S., Short, C., Watkins, C. and Winter, M. (1990a). *The Rural Church: Staff and Buildings* (Cirencester, Rural Church Project).

—— (1990b). *The Clergy Life* (Cirencester, Rural Church Project).

—— (1990c). *Parish Life and Rural Religion* (Cirencester, Rural Church Project).

—— (1990d). *The Views of Rural Parishioners* (Cirencester, Rural Church Project).

Davies, D., Watkins, C. and Winter, M. (1991). *Church and Religion in Rural England* (Edinburgh, T. & T. Clark).

Davies, E. T. (1970). *Disestablishment and Disendowment* (Penarth, Church in Wales Publications).

Davies, J. (1993). *A History of Wales* (London, Allen Lane).

Durkheim, E. (1961). *The Elementary Forms of the Religious Life* (New York, Collier). (First published, Paris, Alcan 1912; first English translation, London, Allen & Unwin, 1915).

Finke, R. and Stark, R. (1992). *The Churching of America 1776–1900* (New Brunswick, NJ, Rutgers University Press).

Freytag, J. (1965). 'The ministry as a profession: a sociological critique', in Paton, D. M. (ed.), *New Forms of Ministry* (London, Edinburgh House).

Giddens, A. (1990). *The Consequences of Modernity* (Oxford, Polity Press).

—— (1994). *Beyond Left and Right: The Future of Radical Politics* (Oxford, Polity Press).

Gilbert, A. D. (1976). *Religion and Society in Industrial England* (London, Longman).

Gill, R. (1993). *The Myth of the Empty Church* (London, SPCK).

Greeley, A. (1992). 'Religion in Britain, Ireland and the USA', chapter 3 in Jowell, R., Brook, L., Prior, G. and Taylor, B. (eds.), *British Social Attitudes: The 9th Report* (Aldershot, Dartmouth).

Hamilton, M. B. (1995). *The Sociology of Religion: Theoretical and Comparative Perspectives* (London, Routledge).

Harris, C. C. (1969). 'Reform in a normative organisation', *Sociological Review*, 17:2, 167–85.

—— (1990a). *The Archbishop's State of the Church Study: Preliminary Report of a Survey of the Province of Wales* (Penarth, Church in Wales Publications).

—— (1990b). 'Religion', in Jenkins, R. and Edwards, A. (eds.), *One Step Forward* (Llandysul, Gomer).

—— (1991). *The Archbishop's State of the Church Study: Report on Phase One Being the Responses of Deaneries and Parishes throughout the Province* (Penarth, Church in Wales Publications).

—— (1993a). *The Archbishop's State of the Church Study: Phase Two, Report of the Survey of the Laity* (Penarth, Church in Wales Publications).

—— (1993b). *The Archbishop's State of the Church Study: Final Report to the Governing Body* (Penarth, Church in Wales Publications).

Harris, C. C. and Startup, R. (1993). 'Lay characteristics and religious attitudes in the Church in Wales', *International Journal of Sociology and Social Policy*, 13:8, 50–66.

—— (1995). 'The Church in Wales: a neglected Welsh institution', *Contemporary Wales*, 7, 97–116.

—— (1996a). 'Clergy activities and attitudes in the Church in Wales', *Research in the Social Scientific Study of Religion*, 7, 109–26.

—— (1996b). 'Is the Church an organization?', Paper given at the

Annual Conference of the Association for the Study of Religion, New York.

—— (1998). 'Researching a traditional territorial organisation: analogy, *Verstehen*, and the sociological imagination', *International Journal of Sociology and Social Policy*, 18:9/10, 72–93.

Hastings, A. (1991). *A History of English Christianity 1920–1990* (London, SCM Press).

Hechter, M. (1975). *Internal Colonialism: The Celtic Fringe in British National Development, 1536–1960* (London, Routledge & Kegan Paul).

Hoge, D. R. (ed.) (1979). *Understanding Church Growth and Decline: 1950–1978* (New York, Pilgrim).

Hornsby-Smith, M. P. (1987). *Roman Catholics in England* (Cambridge, Cambridge University Press).

—— (1989). *The Changing Parish: A Study of Parishes, Priests and Parishioners after Vatican II* (London, Routledge & Kegan Paul).

Iannaccone, L. R. (1994). 'Why strict churches are strong', *American Journal of Sociology*, 99, 1180–211.

Jones, S. H. and Francis, L. J. (1998). 'The fate of the Welsh clergy: an attitude survey among male clerics in the Church in Wales', *Contemporary Wales*, 10, 182–99.

Jowell, R., Witherspoon, S. and Brook, L. (eds.) (1988). *British Social Attitudes: The 5th Report* (Aldershot, Gower Publishing Co.).

Jowell, R., Brook, L., Prior, G. and Taylor, B. (eds.) (1992). *British Social Attitudes: The 9th Report* (Aldershot, Dartmouth).

Jud, G. J. (1970). *E-Pastors* (Philadelphia, Pa., Pilgrim).

Kelley, D. M. (1977). *Why Conservative Churches Are Growing* (New York, Harper & Row).

Lauer, R. H. (1973). 'Organisational punishment: punitive relations in a voluntary association', *Human Relations*, 26, 189–202.

Lenski, G. (1961). *The Religious Factor* (Garden City, NY, Doubleday).

Parsons, T. (1951). *The Social System* (New York, Free Press).

Paul, L. (1964). *The Deployment and Payment of the Clergy* (London, Church Information Office).

Piachaud, D. and Webb, J. (1996). *The Price of Food* (London, STICERD/LSE).

Price, D. T. W. (1990). *A History of the Church in Wales in the Twentieth Century* (Penarth, Church in Wales Publications).

Ranson, S., Bryman, A. and Hinings, B. (1977). *Clergy, Ministers and Priests* (London, Routledge & Kegan Paul).

Richter, P. and Francis, L. J. (1998). *Gone but Not Forgotten: Church Leaving and Return in the Twenty-First Century* (London, Darton, Longman & Todd).

Robertson, R. (1970). *The Sociological Interpretation of Religion* (Oxford, Blackwell).

Rosser, C. and Harris, C. C. (1965). *The Family and Social Change* (London, Routledge & Kegan Paul).

Simon, G. (1970). *Address to the Governing Body of the Church in Wales* (Cardiff, Governing Body of the Church in Wales).

Stark, R. (1996). 'Why religious movements succeed or fail: a revised general mode', *Journal of Contemporary Religion*, 11, 133–46.

Stark, R. and Bainbridge, W. S. (1985). *The Future of Religion: Secularization, Revival and Cult Formation* (Berkeley, University of California Press).

Stark, R. and Iannaccone, L. R. (1997). 'Why the Jehovah's Witnesses grow so rapidly: a theoretical application', *Journal of Contemporary Religion*, 12:2, 133–57.

Startup, R. and Harris, C. C. (1997). 'Elements of religious belief and social values among the laity of the Church in Wales', *Journal of Contemporary Religion*, 12:2, 215–28.

Tamney, J. B. (1992). *The Resilience of Christianity in the Modern World* (Albany, NY, State University of New York Press).

Tamney, J. B. and Johnson, S. D. (1998). 'The popularity of strict churches', *Review of Religious Research*, 39, 209–23.

Thompson, K. A. (1970). *Bureaucracy and Church Reform* (Oxford, Oxford University Press).

Towler, R. and Coxon, A. P. M. (1979). *The Fate of the Anglican Clergy.* (London, Macmillan).

Troeltsch, E. (1981). *The Social Teaching of the Christian Churches*, 2 vols. (Chicago, Ill., University of Chicago Press).

Walker, D. (1976). 'Disestablishment and independence', in Walker, D. (ed.), *A History of the Church in Wales* (Penarth, Church in Wales Publications).

Weber, M. (1965). *The Sociology of Religion* (London, Methuen).

Williams, G. (1991). *The Welsh and their Religion* (Cardiff, University of Wales Press).

Wood, A. H. (ed.) (1987). *The Times Guide to the House of Commons June 1987* (London, Times).

Index of Authors

Index of Subjects

LIBRARY, UNIVERSITY COLLEGE CHESTER